The ENCYCLOPedia of Bible Games

FOR CHILDREN'S MINISTRY

Group

Loveland, Colorado

www.group.com

Group resources actually work!

This Group resource helps you focus on **"The 1 Thing™"**— a life-changing relationship with Jesus Christ. "The 1 Thing" incorporates our **R.E.A.L.** approach to ministry. It reinforces a growing friendship with Jesus, encourages long-term learning, and results in life transformation, because it's:

Relational
Learner-to-learner interaction enhances learning and builds Christian friendships.

Experiential
What learners experience through discussion and action sticks with them up to 9 times longer than what they simply hear or read.

Applicable
The aim of Christian education is to equip learners to be both hearers and doers of God's Word.

Learner-based
Learners understand and retain more when the learning process takes into consideration how they learn best.

The Encyclopedia of Bible Games for Children's Ministry

Visit our Web site: **www.group.com**

Credits
Contributing Authors: Michael Bonner, Teryl Cartwright, John Cutshall, Ruthie Daniels, Enelle Eder, Brooke Gibson, Judy Gillispie, Jan Kershner, Scott Kinner, Katherine Martinez, Julie Meiklejohn, Frieda Nossaman, Christopher Perciante, Karen Schmidt, Christina Schofield, Val Scott, Larry Shallenberger, Alison Simpson, Lyricia Squyres, Bonnie Temple, Jon Woodhams, and Lori Wynn
Editors: Vicki L.O. Witte and Mikal Keefer
Creative Development Editor: Mikal Keefer
Chief Creative Officer: Joani Schultz
Copy Editor: Dena Twinem
Art Director: Kari K. Monson
Cover Art Director: Bambi Eitel
Print Production Artist: Joyce Douglas
Illustrator: Matt Wood
Cover Illustrator: Tracy O'very Covey
Production Manager: Peggy Naylor

Library of Congress Cataloging-in-Publication Data
The encyclopedia of Bible games for children's ministry.--1st American pbk. ed.
    p.   cm.
  Includes indexes.
  ISBN 0-7644-2696-6 (pbk. : alk. paper)
  1. Games in Christian education. 2. Church work with children. 3. Bible games and puzzles. I. Group Publishing.
    BV1536.3E53 2004
    268' .432--dc22

                    2004010539

10 9 8 7 6 5 4 3   13 12 11 10 09 08 07 06
Printed in the United States of America.

Table of Contents

Section 1 Bible Story Games 13

*Bible lessons boring? No way!
Not with these great games that correlate
with major Bible stories!*

2 Section Jesus Is...Games 115

*Here are ten games to help
you connect your kids with Jesus!*

Section 3 The Bible Is...Games 129

*Help kids discover ten truths
about the Bible with these games!*

Section 4 Holiday Games 143

Games for your holiday parties or just for fun!

Section **9** Group Builder Games **235**

Twenty games to help kids form lasting friendships!

Introduction

Games are great—they get kids involved, build relationships, and make coming to church fun.

But you have so little time with your children...do you *really* want to spend it playing games?

Absolutely—because every game you find here reinforces a Bible truth, explores a Bible principle, and cements Bible learning. Your kids will have fun learning Bible stories and Bible themes!

The Encyclopedia of Bible Games for Children's Ministry includes fun, non-competitive Bible games for holidays, icebreakers, group builders, road trips, total silence, and those wild 'n' wacky times. In short, Bible games for any occasion...any energy level...and nearly any Bible story!

Use the helpful indexes to find the perfect game to complement your Bible lesson. You can search by Scripture reference, the game's energy level (low, medium, or high), or by the name of the game. It's easy to find the perfect game for your group to enjoy!

Keep this book handy—you'll use it often! It's a game-time lifesaver for Sunday school, midweek programs and clubs, camps, retreats, road trips, and seasonal programs.

Get ready to have some fun!

How to adapt games for your unique situation

Have a small group?

No problem! Most games that call for groups can be played by individuals, or by having your entire class work together as one group. We've built in flexibility so you can play it by ear when you see how many kids show up.

Want to modify games to fit your kids' abilities?

It's easy! If you have younger children, give them added advantages—a head start, shorter or smaller goals, or bonus points awarded right up front. With older kids, give them added challenges—announce they have to play blindfolded, hopping on one foot, or with one hand behind their backs. For a group of mixed ages, it's OK to use *both* these strategies in order to even up the game for all the children to enjoy.

Have space limitations?

See a game that sounds great to play outdoors but you only have a small indoor space? Consider having the children crawl on their knees or walk like crabs instead of running, and you can play most any game indoors.

Two game-safety considerations

A few of these games use food. It's important to know if any of the children you work with has a dangerous food allergy—consult with parents about allergies their children may have. Also be sure to carefully read food labels, as hidden ingredients can cause allergy-related problems.

Some games use blindfolds. Please use only *clean* blindfolds. Be sure the blindfolds have been washed since the last time your kids used them to prevent the spread of eye infections, and that the blindfolds weren't once used to wipe up food spills or as shop rags.

Feel free to get creative about using dish towels, bandannas, scarves, and neckties for blindfolds—but please make sure they're clean!

Section

Bible Story Games

Bible lessons boring? No way! Not with these great games that correlate with major Bible stories!

ABCs of Creation

(God Creates the World)

Genesis 1:1–2:3
Energy Level
Low Energy
This game will help your kids be creative in thinking about the things that God created.

Supply List
☐ none needed

The Game

Have the children sit down in a circle. Then say: **Today we'll think about things that God created using the letters of the alphabet as our guide. I will begin the game by saying, "God created the earth and he made Adam." The person next to me will then say, "God created the earth and he made Adam and** [something that starts with the letter B]." We'll keep going around the circle, repeating the things that God made for each letter, and adding one more for the next. If you get stuck, the rest of us will help you.**

If you have more than twenty-six children, divide the class into smaller groups so that each child will get to say something for a letter of the alphabet. If you have fewer than twenty-six children, each child can take as many turns as needed to complete the entire alphabet.

Post-Game Discussion Questions

After playing this game, discuss these questions with your students:

• **How does it feel to know that God created so many different things? Why?**

• **What do you think was the most amazing thing God created? Why?**

• **How can we thank God for his creation?**

Say: **Let's close in prayer and thank God for all the wonderful things he created.**

Name Tag

(God Creates Adam and Eve)

Genesis 2:4-22

Energy Level

High Energy

This game will help your kids appreciate the value and presence of every individual in your group—as they explore the story of Adam and Eve.

Supply List

❑ none needed

The Game

Greet and gather your group, and say: **When you spend time with people, you get to know them better. God spent time each day with Adam and Eve, and he knew all their special qualities. Let's spend some time getting to know** *each other.* **When your turn comes, please give your name and describe something special about yourself. Listen carefully—you may need to know this information!** Explain that it's easier to remember someone's name if you know something about him or her. Start by introducing yourself, so the kids have an example to follow.

Once everyone has been introduced, say: **We're going to play chain tag with a twist.** Explain that as people are tagged by whoever is "It," they join hands with the chain of captives and help tag others.

Say: **Here's the twist: In order to keep someone you have tagged, you must say that person's name and declare his or her special quality. For example, if I'm "It" and I touch Samantha, I grab her hand and say real loud, "This is Samantha and she was born in Alabama."**

If the taggers fail to introduce you accurately, you can introduce yourself again. Next time you're tagged, we'll definitely remember your name!

Post-Game Discussion Questions

After playing this game, ask your students to sit down in groups of three and discuss:

• **What did you learn about the people in our group?**

• **Why did God create Adam and Eve? How were they special?**

• **Why did God create** *you***? How did God make** *you* **special?**

Say: **God creates each person with special and unique qualities. He takes the time to know us, and he appreciates our differences.**

Silent Snake Tag

(Adam and Eve Sin)

Genesis 3:1-24

Energy Level

Low Energy

This game will help your students practice listening for "trouble" and staying away from it.

Supply List

❑ classroom table

❑ two clean cloth blindfolds

❑ piece of fruit (real, artificial, or cut from construction paper)

The Game

Remove any chairs from around the table. Then have the kids stand in a big circle around the table far enough back so that no one can touch the table. Say: **The snake tricked Adam and Eve into doing something wrong. He was sneaky and tried to cause trouble!**

Adam and Eve both should have stayed away from that snake. Let's play a game where you listen carefully for the "snake" and try not to get caught.

Choose two volunteers to begin, one as the snake and one as Adam (if a boy) or Eve (if a girl). Blindfold both, and give the fruit to the snake. Both players should stand touching the table on opposite sides.

The child playing the snake will sneak around the table trying to tag "Adam" or "Eve" with the fruit, while the child playing Adam or Eve listens carefully to hear when the snake is coming and moves away. Both players must keep at least one hand on the table at all times. They may change direction at any time but may not crawl over or under the table. The kids watching will impersonate the sound of other animals that might have been in the Garden of Eden. Allow kids to select their own animals to mimic.

Set a time limit, such as thirty seconds, to play. The first round ends when the snake tags Adam or Eve or time runs out. Then choose two different kids to play. If you have a large group, set up multiple tables at which to play.

Post-Game Discussion Questions

After playing this game, ask your students to sit in small groups and discuss:

• Was it easy or hard to stay away from trouble in this game? Why?

• How is that like real life? How is it different?

• Why do you think it's important to try to stay away from trouble or temptation?

• What kinds of things would help us say no to temptation?

Say: **If we stay alert and watch out for temptation each day, we'll be better prepared to recognize it and stay away!**

Puzzled and Mixed Up

(Noah Builds the Ark)

Genesis 6:5-22

Energy Level

Low Energy

In this game, your students will identify with Noah the ark-builder as they work with their friends to complete a challenging task.

Supply List

❑ several boxed animal puzzles—of similar size and difficulty (twenty-five to one hundred pieces, depending on the ages of your students)

❑ a tub or box—large enough to hold all the puzzle pieces

The Game

After you've greeted your students, hold up a stack of boxed puzzles and ask:

• **Who can help me open the puzzles and dump them in this tub?**

Distribute the boxes to volunteers, and have them open the puzzles and dump the pieces in the tub. Invite several others to thoroughly mix the contents of the tub!

Say: **Noah obeyed God when he built a huge boat and gathered the** animals as God had instructed him. Our task is to assemble all these animal puzzles. We'll work in groups to sort the pieces and complete all the puzzles.

Divide your students into groups of approximately equal size, and assign each group one puzzle to assemble. Observe your students' progress and intermittently offer hints like these: "Cooperate with the other groups to sort all the pieces before you begin" or "Work on the corners and edges first."

Give the children a time limit based on how much time you have available; for example, you might let them work for between five and fifteen minutes.

Post-Game Discussion Questions

When all the puzzles are finished, or the time is up, congratulate your students for their fine work. Then have them sit down with their groups and discuss these questions:

• **How did it feel to assemble this puzzle with the help of your group? What was hardest? easiest?**

• **What would it feel like to sort and assemble all the puzzles alone? Why?**

• **What kind of help or support did Noah receive when he built and launched the ark?**

Say: **God trusts us and gives us big assignments sometimes. Thankfully, he does not expect us to complete them all alone! God gives us faithful people who help.**

How Much Farther?

(God Floods the Earth)

Genesis 7:1–8:22; 9:8-16

Energy Level

Low Energy

This travel game will teach your students perspective—as they estimate travel times and explore the experiences of Noah and his passengers.

Supply List

☐ a wristwatch or reliable vehicle clock

☐ pencils and paper

☐ road atlas (optional)

☐ a supply of small rewards such as healthy snacks, coloring sheets and crayons, tiny notepads and stickers (optional)

The Game

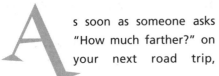

As soon as someone asks "How much farther?" on your next road trip, launch this game by saying: **Journeys can be long, and it's hard to wait! I wonder how Noah felt as he and his companions waited for the flood to end and the earth to dry out? Let's play a guessing game that will make this trip fly by. It's called "How Much Farther?"**

Divide the travelers into pairs or trios. Briefly describe the scope of your journey, and name some towns or landmarks on the route. Have each group locate the landmarks on the map, if possible.

Say: **Discuss with your group how many minutes it will take to reach the first landmark.** Have the groups record their guesses. When all groups are ready, have them share their guesses aloud. **Once we reach this landmark, we'll celebrate your great guesses with a treat!**

When you reach the landmark, notice the time and compare it with kids' guesses. Have kids share how they arrived at their estimates. Celebrate their participation with a simple treat, and say: **Great work! Let's look at the map and guess the time to our next landmark.**

Post-Game Discussion Questions

After you've passed three or four landmarks, congratulate your travelers, and discuss these questions:

• What factors did you consider when you made your guesses?

• Which were your best guesses? Why?

• How do you think Noah might have felt as he waited for the floodwaters to recede? Explain.

• What method did Noah use to check on his progress?

Say: **It feels great to arrive at your destination after a long, challenging journey. Noah was faithful and patient. He did what God asked him to, and God kept Noah safe and dry.**

No Babble Babel

(People Build a Tower at Babel)

Genesis 11:1-9

Energy Level

Medium Energy

This silent game will prompt your kids toward creative communication and cooperation as they work together to build a tower.

Supply List

☐ a large tub of building blocks—any sort of stackable blocks will work, but have *lots* of them!

The Game

Warmly welcome your kids, and point out your large supply of blocks. Ask: **If we were to build a tower with these objects, how tall do you think we could go?** Encourage the students to offer guesses, then say: **Let's work together to build a tower, but let's do it in total silence!**

Explain that no one may talk or communicate in any way—including gestures. Once the tower is finished, help the kids estimate the height of the tower. Then say: **Let's build it again, and this time one person in the class may communicate through gestures.** Help the students decide who may gesture. Build your tower and estimate its height.

Finish your game with a final round. Say: **Let's build one last tower. This time anyone may gesture, but still—no talking!** When the tower is finished, estimate the height.

Post-Game Discussion Questions

After you've finished the game, draw the kids together, and discuss these questions:

• **How did it feel to work together without talking? Why?**

• **In what ways did the use of gestures make your task easier? How did the gestures make it more confusing?**

• **How did God hinder the progress of the tower-builders at Babel?**

• **Why did God want to stop them?**

Say: **Everything is easier when people speak the same language!**

Build It With the Blueprints

(Abram Follows God's Direction)

Genesis 12:1-8
Energy Level

Medium Energy

This game will help your kids understand the value of helpful direction as they work together to build something fun.

Supply List

❑ two or more identical sets of building materials such as Lincoln Logs, Tinkertoys, or Lego construction toys

❑ copies of a pictured structure that can be built with the pieces provided (from the toy leaflet)

❑ copies of the written directions for building the pictured structure (from the toy leaflet)

The Game

Greet your students warmly, and divide them into groups based on the size of your class and the number of building sets you have available. Hold up one of the building sets and say: **We're going to work together in groups to build this** [show the picture and name the structure you are building].

Explain to the students that you are adding a twist to the project. Say: **God told Abram to leave his home and travel to a new land. Along the way, God gave Abram simple instructions to guide him on the journey.**

I'm providing half the groups with this picture of the [name the structure]. **The other group(s) will have the picture plus written directions.** Encourage the kids to have fun building the toy, whether they are following directions or inventing the steps themselves while looking at the picture.

Post-Game Discussion Questions

When the structures are finished, bring the groups together to discuss these questions.

• **What were the difficulties for the group(s) that built the** [name the structure] **without directions?**

• **How did the directions help the group(s) that had them?**

• **What directions did Abram receive from God? How might Abram's life have been different if he had been without these instructions?**

Say: **God always gives helpful direction when he asks us to accomplish difficult things.**

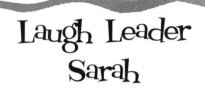

Laugh Leader Sarah

(Isaac Is Born)

Genesis 21:1-6
Energy Level
Medium Energy
This game will help students recognize God's gift of laughter and the benefits of sharing it together.

Supply List
☐ none needed

The Game

Send a few students out of the room to wait quietly until you call them back inside. After they've left, pick one person to be "Sarah, the Laugh Leader." Instruct kids who've remained in the room to walk around, laughing. They've got to secretly watch "Sarah," because when "Sarah" stops laughing, everyone must stop laughing—though they'll all continue walking around the room.

Ask the other students to come back in the room and walk around with the laughing students, watching everyone carefully. When all the students stop laughing because "Sarah" has stopped, ask the students observing to each guess which child is "Sarah, the Laugh Leader." Whoever these students choose must tell whether or not they are "Sarah" and then each share one thing that makes him or her laugh.

Play several rounds, as time allows, sending different children out of the room and choosing a new "Sarah" each time.

Post-Game Discussion Questions

After playing this game, ask your students to sit down and discuss:

• **How did you know who "Sarah" was?**

• **What are some other ways besides laughter that we can tell someone is happy?**

• **Why is it better to laugh *with* someone than *at* someone?**

No Lie!

(Jacob's Deception)

Genesis 25:27-34; 27:1-40

Energy Level

Low Energy

Your kids will become better acquainted as they play this game—sharing truths about themselves and exploring the story of Jacob's deception.

Supply List

❏ none needed

The Game

Warmly greet the children, and gather them into a circle. Say: **Let's begin our time by sharing some interesting facts about ourselves.** Explain to the kids that a fact is something that is true. **For example, I was born in** [name your birthplace]. Give the students a moment to think of a fact that they might share. Encourage them to pick something that others probably don't know.

Say: **Let's add a twist to our game.** Have the students imagine an untruth—or lie—about themselves. **For example, I once visited** [name a destination to which you've never been]. Give the students some time to think of a lie about themselves.

When everyone is ready, take turns sharing your fact and your lie. As each person shares, allow the group to guess which statement is true and which is false. Encourage the kids to be creative in their bluffing!

Post-Game Discussion Questions

When the game is finished, have a group discussion, using these questions as a guide:

• **How did you feel as you told the lie about yourself? Why?**

• **How could you determine whether someone was lying or telling the truth?**

• **What lies did Jacob tell his father about himself?**

• **Why did Jacob lie?**

Say: **Every person is valuable to God. Sometimes we forget this truth, and we're tempted to bluff or lie about our qualities or experiences. The truth is, God and others appreciate us just the way we are.**

From Smirk to Smile

(Joseph's Disturbing Dreams)

Genesis 37:1-11

Energy Level

Low Energy

This game will help your kids explore some of the emotions that Joseph's brothers experienced in reaction to his dreams.

Supply List

☐ none needed

The Game

Have the students form a circle. Their goal is to keep frowns on their faces while, one by one, chosen students come up to them and say, "Listen to this dream I had. I dreamed that..."

The student in the middle must finish the sentence and use only his or her voice to try to draw out the desired smile. If the "target" student smiles, then the two students trade places. If there is no smile, the student must move on to tell another student about a different dream. The game ends when all have had a chance at both Frowner and Dream-Teller or when time runs out.

Post-Game Discussion Questions

After playing this game, ask your students to sit down in groups of three and discuss:

• Joseph's brothers weren't very happy about his dreams; how do you react when people tell you their dreams?

• What was the funniest dream you ever had?

• Have you ever had a dream come true? Tell about it.

Say: **Dreams can be funny or they can be scary. Sometimes God even uses dreams to tell us his plans.**

I've Got a Deal for You, Brother!

(Joseph's Brothers Sell Him)

Genesis 37:12-36
Energy Level

High Energy

Your kids will understand what kind of mood Joseph's brothers were in as they play this game and explore what the brothers had in mind for Joseph.

Supply List

❑ enough colored (wrapped) candies, beads, or marbles for every student to have ten

❑ small plastic bag or envelope for each child (to hold the items)

The Game

Give each student ten candies (or marbles or beads) of varying colors plus a plastic bag or envelope to hold them in. Say: **The goal of this game is to end up with ten candies** [marbles, beads] **of the same color. The way to do that is by following these simple steps. Each of you will decide how many candies** [marbles, beads] **you want to trade, and hide no more than three in your hand. Remember, you are only allowed to trade up to three candies** [marbles, beads] **at a time. You then begin to shout the number of candies** [marbles, beads] **you wish to trade. When you find someone who is shouting the same number as you are, stop shouting; say, "I've got a deal for you, brother"; and make the trade. You must give that person all of the candies** [marbles, beads] **you have in your hand and you must take all the marbles the other person has in his or her hand regardless of color. No picking and choosing is allowed. Once you have all ten candies** [marbles, beads] **of the same color, yell, "The market is closed!"**

Post-Game Discussion Questions

After playing this game, ask your students to sit down in groups of three and discuss:

• Joseph's brothers sold him to a caravan of traders. What have you ever sold or traded to another person?

• What would happen if you found someone who was interested in buying your brother or sister? How would your parents react?

• Have you ever made a deal with someone and then wished you hadn't? Tell about it.

Say: **Joseph's brothers weren't very kind in their actions, but stories that start out bad don't always end up that way. God can use even the strangest things for his purposes.**

You're Forgiven Tag

(Joseph Forgives His Brothers)

Genesis 42:1–45:28
Energy Level

High Energy
This game will help your kids discover the need for forgiveness in their lives.

Supply List

☐ room or outdoor space large enough for a game of tag

The Game

Choose a student to be The Freezer. The Freezer tries to tag other players. Once a child is tagged, she or he must "freeze" in place. Frozen children may attract other players' attention by shouting, "Forgive me!" The only way to re-enter the game is for another child to touch a frozen player and say, "You are forgiven." If a child is frozen three times, she or he then becomes The Freezer, and the game continues. Play as long as time allows.

Post-Game Discussion Questions

After the game, have children be seated, and discuss these questions:

• **Have you ever needed forgiveness before in your life? What happened?**

• **Why is it often more difficult to forgive someone than to receive forgiveness?**

• **Why is it that when you need forgiveness, you feel all frozen inside?**

• **Why is it that after you are forgiven, you feel so free?**

Say: **Just as you needed "forgiveness" to stay in the game, Joseph's brothers needed real-life forgiveness to keep moving in their lives too!**

Wrapping Baby Moses

(God Protects Moses)

Exodus 1:1–2:10

Energy Level

Medium Energy

This game will help your kids discover the incredible act of faith that Moses' mother demonstrated in hiding her baby among the reeds of the Nile to save him from certain death.

Supply List

☐ one baby doll

☐ one basket or box large enough to hold the baby doll

☐ one baby blanket or bath towel

The Game

Say: **Let's play a game that will help us understand what Moses' mother must have gone through when she hid her baby Moses in the reeds of the Nile River to** save him from Pharaoh.

Have the kids form two parallel lines, facing each other, on opposite sides of the room. Designate one line the Wrappers and the other line the Unwrappers. Lay the doll, a blanket, and the basket next to each other in the middle of the space between the two lines.

Say: **The first person in the Wrappers line will run out to the baby, wrap it tightly in the blanket, place it in the basket, and run back to the line. Then the first person in the Unwrappers line will run out to where the baby is lying, unwrap the doll, and place the blanket, doll, and basket where you see them right now. Whenever someone returns to his or her line, the next person in the other line may go. We're racing against the clock!**

After giving the directions, start the lines running. Make sure each child has a turn to do the activity. Once everyone in both lines has gone, switch which line wraps and which unwraps. To add urgency you may time the two lines combined to determine how long it takes to accomplish the task. See if teams can complete the second round in less time.

Post-Game Discussion Questions

After playing this game, ask your students to sit down in groups of three and discuss:

• **How do you think Moses' mother must have felt when Pharaoh ordered the death of every newborn male? Explain.**

• **Describe how you felt as you were hurrying to take care of the baby. How was this like or unlike how Moses'** mom must have felt when she had to let Moses go in a basket in the river?

• **How was Moses' mother showing trust in God when she placed baby Moses in a basket and laid him in the Nile River?**

Say: **God protected Moses by giving his mom faith, and by giving his mom the chance to care for Moses even after the baby was discovered by Pharaoh's daughter.**

Reveal the Light

(Moses and the Burning Bush)

Exodus 2:11–3:20

Energy Level

High Energy

This game will help your kids understand that God revealed himself to Moses through the light of fire as you explore together the story of Moses and the burning bush.

Supply List

☐ flashlight

The Game

Play this game in a large, dark room or in a large outdoor area after dark.

To begin, ask students to brainstorm some ideas about what it *means* to follow God and what it's *like* to follow God. Students might say things like "It's sometimes tough to follow God" or "I try to follow God all the time."

Give one student a flashlight, and explain that he or she is "It." Don't use a super high-powered flashlight—a smaller or weaker one will actually work better for this game. The group will play a game of tag in which "It" tries to "tag" others by shining the flashlight on them. Give the group to the count of five to scatter, then begin the game. When a person is tagged, he or she should "freeze" and call out one of the ideas about following God, then continue play. Continue until "It" becomes tired, then have "It" choose a new person to be "It."

Post-Game Discussion Questions

After playing this game, have students sit in a circle and discuss:

• **How did you feel when you saw the light coming for you? Explain.**

• **How do you think Moses must have felt when he saw the burning bush? Why?**

• **How does God reveal himself to you?**

• **How can you follow God?**

Say: **Moses encountered God in a big, miraculous way, and his life was never the same. Moses committed his life to God and followed him for the rest of his life. In the same way, God wants to reveal himself to us, and he wants us to commit our lives to following him.**

Scrambled Plagues

(Moses Pleads With Pharaoh)

Exodus 7:14–12:30

Energy Level

High Energy

This game will help your kids discover or review the plagues God used to convince Pharaoh to let his people go.

Supply List

❑ none needed

The Game

Say: **When God was ready to lead the Israelites out of Egypt, he sent Moses to tell Pharaoh to let his people go. Each time Pharaoh said "no," God sent another plague on the land. Does anyone remember some of the plagues God sent?** Give kids a chance to respond, and then remind them of any plagues they couldn't remember. The plagues included: the Nile River turned to blood, frogs everywhere, gnats, flies, dead livestock, boils, hail, locusts, darkness, and death to the firstborn Egyptian males.

We're going to play a wild game to help us remember God's power in freeing his people from Egypt.

Have each child choose one of the plagues. If you have more than ten children, it's fine to have more than one child choose the same plague. Have the children sit on the floor in a circle, with one child in the middle. The child in the middle should call out two or three plagues. All the kids who have chosen those plagues, plus the child in the middle, must stand and race for the empty spaces where other children were seated. seats. The child left standing is the new middle child. If a child calls out "All ten plagues!" all the children must race for new seats. Play several rounds, until each child has been in the middle, if possible.

Post-Game Discussion Questions

After playing this game, ask your students to sit down in groups of three and discuss:

• How would you have felt if you were an Egyptian person facing such terrible plagues? Explain.

• Why do you think Pharaoh was so slow to let the Israelites go even after God struck the Egyptians with so many plagues?

• Describe a time that we sometimes don't do what God wants us to do no matter how many times he urges us to do the right thing.

Say: **God never forgot his people when they were slaves in Egypt. God is so powerful that he can use even mighty plagues to change the mind of a hardhearted Pharaoh. God's power over Pharaoh shows us that he can help us in difficult circumstances too.**

Silent Crossing
(Crossing the Red Sea)

Exodus 13:17–14:31
Energy Level
Medium Energy

In this game your students will explore what the Israelites may have felt when crossing the Red Sea.

Supply List
☐ clean cloth blindfolds, enough for half the children

The Game

Have your students form two groups of equal size. One group will be the "Red Sea" and the other group will be "Egyptians." Say: **The goal of this game is for the Egyptians to get from one side of the Red Sea to the other without being washed away. The Egyptians must sneak through the Red Sea without being touched. Those playing the Red Sea must choose a place to stand and plant their feet. The catch is that even though the Red Sea may have teeth, it has no eyes. Everyone in** the Red Sea group will be blindfolded.

Let the Red Sea group scatter themselves across the room and put on their blindfolds. Remind them that they must keep their feet planted as they try to catch the Egyptians.

Let the Egyptians try to sneak, rush, or wind their way through the Red Sea. If they are touched, they must go back and try again. After a few minutes, have a changing of the tide...in other words, have the kids switch groups. Let the Red Sea become the Egyptians and the Egyptians become the Red Sea, and repeat the game.

Post-Game Discussion Questions

After the game, have the children sit down and discuss these questions:

• **Why was it hard to avoid being tagged by the Red Sea?**

• **The Egyptians were a mighty army, and yet they were powerless against the Red Sea. Why?**

• **Have you ever been underwater and needed a breath of air? Tell us about it.**

Say: **You may have found it hard to be the Red Sea in this game. But remember, God controls the sea and used it to destroy the Egyptian army.**

Beach Ball Madness

(The Ten Commandments)

Exodus 19:16–20:21

Energy Level

Medium Energy

This game will help your kids discover that life is much easier with guidelines, rules, and standards such as the Ten Commandments.

Supply List

❑ one beach ball or a kick ball for every six kids

The Game

Have groups of about six children form circles. Say: **OK, I think everyone is ready to play the game. Ready, go!** After saying "go," toss a beach ball into each circle without any further instructions. Let the kids bounce the ball around and grumble for a few moments about not knowing what to do.

Then give children the actual instructions for the game. Say: **It seems no one knew how to play this game. The person in each group that is holding the ball right now must make** an easy toss to another person in the circle. That person then makes a toss to a different person in the circle. Do that until each person has had a turn to catch and toss the ball. The order in which you tossed the ball is the pattern you must follow. Continue to toss the ball in that order.

Once kids have their patterns established, let them repeat the pattern several times. You can make the game more challenging by having each group toss two balls around the pattern.

Post-Game Discussion Questions

After playing this game, ask your students to sit down in their groups and discuss:

• How did it feel when you were told to start a game without any instructions? Explain.

• Why do rules and guidelines help to make games more fun?

• How are the Ten Commandments like rules to a game?

• How do the Ten Commandments make it easier to live with other people?

Say: **The Ten Commandments are rules that help us have a better relationship with God and with each other. Playing by the rules helps everyone get along better.**

Spies and Giants

(Spies Into the Promised Land)

Numbers 13:1–14:23

Energy Level

High Energy
This game of hide-and-seek with soft foam balls will help your kids appreciate the courage that God gave Joshua and Caleb as they explored the Promised Land.

Supply List

❑ soft foam balls—one for each player

The Game

Choose an indoor or outdoor setting that would work for a tag-type game. Determine safe boundaries, and identify a remote area for the "spies' camp." Gather your group, and say: **We're going to play tag—with foam balls.**

Explain that half the group will be "spies" and half will be "giants." The giants have two minutes to go out in pairs and hide from the spies. Help your students form groups of spies and giants, and carefully communicate the boundaries of the game.

Say: **Spies, after two minutes, you will try to capture the giants by tossing foam balls at them. If a giant is touched by a foam ball, that giant is considered captured and you can take the giant back to the spies' camp. Giants can be freed from "prison" if another giant makes his or her way safely to the camp and hits a captured giant with a foam ball.**

Send the spies to their camp, and the giants off to hide. After two minutes, let the game begin. When all the giants are captured, or after a certain amount of time, have the kids switch roles and play again.

Post-Game Discussion Questions

After playing this game, ask your students to sit down in groups of three and discuss:

• **How did it feel to venture out as a spy? Why?**

• **What strategies did spies use to capture giants?**

• **Why were Joshua and Caleb unafraid—and willing to explore and take the Promised Land—even though the people there were giants?**

Say: **God gives us strength and courage to tackle big problems—and big adventures!**

Furry Friends and Friendly Faces

(Balaam's Donkey Talks)

Numbers 22:1-38

Energy Level

Low Energy

This travel game encourages kids to describe the important people in their lives and appreciate God's creative power.

Supply List

☐ none needed

The Game

When your kids begin to tire of a road trip, bring up the story of Balaam and his donkey. Say: **It's fun to discover how creative God is in the ways he designs and communicates with his creation!**

I know a fun game that will pass the time and help us celebrate God's creativity. Explain that each person will have a turn to describe the good qualities of a family member or close friend. Once the description is complete, fellow travelers can ask questions about the person.

Once we've heard about your loved one, we'll think of an animal that symbolizes this person. For example, a strong, brave person reminds us of a horse while a fun, playful person resembles an otter. It's fun to offer several suggestions, narrowing the discussion until the person is excited about an animal that represents his or her family member.

Encourage your carload to offer positive descriptions and flattering animal associations! Keep the game moving with a creative method for taking turns. For example, the person owning the most fish might begin.

Post-Game Discussion Questions

After everyone has had a turn, discuss these questions:

• **How has God used these people to communicate with you and teach you about him?**

• **Why would God use a donkey to communicate with Balaam?**

Say: **Everyone and everything on earth belongs to God. Sometimes God uses unusual methods to communicate with us, especially when he has something important to say!**

The Walls Fall Down

(God Gives Victory Over Jericho)

Joshua 6:1-27
Energy Level

Medium Energy
This game will help your kids experience the victory that God gave to Joshua and the Israelites at Jericho.

Supply List

☐ lots of building blocks or empty boxes, at least one per child (the bigger the blocks, the bigger the wall!)

The Game

Have students stand in a circle and number off. Place the pile of blocks in the center of the circle, and designate an area where students will build the wall. Explain that you will call out numbers, and every child with one of those numbers should run to the pile of blocks, pick up one block, and add it to the wall. When you're out of blocks and all the children have had a turn, march around the wall together noisily. Then allow the children to knock down the wall with cheers and shouts.

Say: **God gave Joshua and the Israelites victory over Jericho. They could not have knocked down the walls without God.**

Post-Game Discussion Questions

After playing this game, ask your students to sit down in groups of three and discuss:

• **How did it feel to march around the wall and knock it down? Why?**

• **How do you think the Israelites must have felt when they saw God knock down the walls around the city of Jericho? Why?**

• **How do you think the people of Jericho felt to see their walls fall down? Why?**

• **What is one difficult situation that you need God to help you have victory over?**

Say: **God can help us have victory over difficult situations, just as he helped Joshua and the Israelites have victory over Jericho.**

Power Building

(God Gives

Gideon Victory)

Judges 6:1-16; 7:1-24

Energy Level

Low Energy

This game will help your kids understand that true power and victory come from God as they explore the story of Gideon.

Supply List

❑ small building blocks, enough for each student to have ten

❑ deck of playing cards with the jokers removed

The Game

Give each student ten blocks. Tell students that the object of this game is to build the tallest tower. Then explain that students will take turns drawing cards from the deck. If a person draws a black card, he or she can take that number of blocks from other players and use them to make his or her tower taller. If a person draws a red card, he or she must give away that number of blocks to other players. Point out that face cards (jacks, queens, and kings) are worth ten, and aces are worth one.

Choose a person to go first; play

should go clockwise from the first person. Continue in this manner until everyone has had at least two turns. If someone runs out of blocks, he or she can still draw a card and take blocks from other people if he or she draws a black card.

Post-Game Discussion Questions

After playing the game, gather students together to discuss these questions:

• How did it feel to try to build your tower? Do you feel like you were successful? Why or why not?

• How do you think Gideon and his men felt when God kept taking power and strength—and soldiers—away from them?

• How do you think they felt at the end of the story when God worked through them to bring about a victory?

• Is it easy or difficult to rely on God? Explain.

Say: **In this game, just as you felt you were doing well, something took all of your "power" away. In the story of Gideon, God took away many things that would have made Gideon powerful. But he made Gideon and his men victorious anyway. God did this because God wanted Gideon and his men, as well as their enemies, to remember that true power and victory come only from God, not from anything people can do or have.**

Super Strength

(God Gives Samson Strength)

Judges 15:9-16; 16:4-30
Energy Level
High Energy
This game will help your students realize that God gives us strength as they play tag and learn about Samson.

Supply List
☐ two CD players ready to play two different upbeat songs

The Game

Gather your group in a large open space. Warmly greet the kids, and say: **We're going to spread out and play a game of freeze tag.** Help the group decide who will begin as "It," and say: **If you are tagged by the person who is "It," you must freeze until someone else touches and frees you.**

Explain that you will be playing music during the game. Play an excerpt from the first song and say:

When this song is playing, the person who is "It" will have normal strength to tag and freeze people. Now play the second song and say: **When this song is playing, "It" will have super strength, like Samson. When "It" has super strength, everyone except for "It" must play the game on one foot!**

Once the instructions are clear, begin the normal-strength song. As the game progresses, switch between the songs, using the volume knobs. Change who's "It" by stopping the music and calling out the name of a new child to fill the job. Try to play the game until everyone has experienced being "It." If your group is large, use several taggers in each game.

Post-Game Discussion Questions

After playing this game, ask your students to sit down in groups of three and discuss:

• **How did it feel to be "It" with normal strength? Why?**

• **What was it like with super strength? Explain.**

• **Why was Samson stronger than other men?**

• **Where did Samson get his strength?**

Say: **God gives amazing strength to his devoted followers.**

Grain Game

(Ruth Trusts God)

Ruth 2:1-12

Energy Level

Medium Energy

This game will help students understand how Ruth trusted God to take care of her, and how your kids can trust God too.

Supply List

❑ one roll of pennies

❑ one small plastic resealable bag for every two kids

❑ one clean cloth blindfold (clean bandannas work well) for every two kids

The Game

Ask students to form pairs, and give each pair a blindfold. Explain that in the Bible story of Ruth, Ruth had to go to the fields to glean, or gather, grain. She had to trust God to help her find enough grain so she and Naomi would have food. Say that in this game, partners will have to trust each other in order to gather "grain." The role of grain will be filled by pennies.

Have partners decide who will be the Gleaner and who will be the Director. Have the Gleaner in each pair wear the blindfold and hold a plastic bag. Clear the center of your room of obstacles, and sprinkle pennies all over the area. Explain that at your signal, the Gleaners should drop to their knees and await instructions from the Directors. The Directors can tell the Gleaners where the "grain" is and how to avoid other Gleaners, but they may not touch the Gleaners at any point.

Let the Gleaners gather grain for several minutes, then call time. The Gleaners should show their bags to their partners, then sprinkle the pennies on the floor again. Have partners switch roles and play again. After calling time again, have kids help you clean up all the pennies from the floor. Put the pennies in the offering.

Post-Game Discussion Questions

After playing the game, ask your students to sit down with their partners and discuss:

• **What was it like to have to trust your partner to tell you where the grain was? Explain.**

• **How is that like how Ruth had to trust God to give her enough grain for food?**

• **When is a time that it's hard for you to trust God? How can the story of Ruth remind you of how God cares for us?**

Encourage kids to remember how God took care of Ruth, and assure them that they, too, can trust God in every situation.

Look and Listen

(Samuel Listens to God)

1 Samuel 3:1-21

Energy Level

Medium Energy

This game will help your kids discover the value of careful listening as they work together and explore the story of Samuel hearing God.

Supply List

☐ a button, penny, or other small object

☐ CD player and CD or radio

☐ bookmarks, healthy snacks, or other simple surprises (optional)

The Game

Before your meeting begins, hide a small object in the meeting place. As your students arrive, greet them warmly, and say: **I've hidden a button in the room and your job is to find it.** Explain that the button won't be easy to find and they may need clues! **You must listen carefully in order to hear the clues.** Tell the kids that music will be playing during the search. No one will know when you are going to offer the clues, and they must hear them amidst the music.

Help your kids divide into pairs or small teams for the search, and encourage them to cooperate in the task. For example, someone might want to concentrate on hearing the clues while his or her partner searches intently.

Give general—not specific—clues. For instance, if the button is near a clock, you might say, "I've got to *hand* it to you, you're good searchers."

Provide the students with a goal. You might say, "Our goal is to the find the button within three clues!" Play the game until the class succeeds, and celebrate with a simple surprise to enjoy as students debrief.

Post-Game Discussion Questions

After playing this game, ask your students to sit down in small groups and discuss:

• **How did the noise affect your ability to hear the clues?**

• **How did you overcome the noise?**

• **How did Samuel know when God was speaking to him?**

• **How can we learn to hear God's voice?**

Say: **God speaks to people in quiet and creative ways. When we tune out earthly noise, it's easier to hear God's voice.**

Crowning the King

(David Becomes King)

1 Samuel 16:1-13

Energy Level

Medium Energy

As your students play a game about David being anointed king over Israel, they'll learn God cares more about their hearts than their outward appearance.

Supply List

☐ a bag of props, including such miscellaneous supplies as toilet paper, tape, streamers, colored paper, cotton balls, markers, stickers, rubber bands, old tablecloths, old clothes, fabric scraps, yarn, and so on

☐ CD player and CD with upbeat music

The Game

s the children arrive, welcome each one into the "castle." Help them form groups of five or six children each. Then say: **Today we'll crown a king—or queen—for each of our teams. Once each team has chosen its royalty, I will give you further instructions.**

Allow just a minute or so for each team to select one student to "anoint" as the king or queen. Be sure to explain the term "anoint" to the group. In Bible times special oil was used to identify, or set apart, an important person such as a king.

Next, show the children your pile of props. Tell them that each group must decorate its royalty using only the supplies provided. Their task is to make the king or queen look as regal as possible using what they have available. Give them ample space to decorate their kings and queens, and about five to ten minutes to work. Play some fast-paced music while the groups are "designing" their royalty.

Have a parade of kings and queens when time is up so each group can see the handiwork of the other teams.

Post-Game Discussion Questions

After playing this game, ask your students to sit down and discuss:

• Why did you choose the person you did to become king or queen?

• Now that you have completed the task, would someone else have made a better king or queen for your group? Explain.

Compare the process teams went through in choosing the royalty with the process Samuel went through in choosing David. Ask:

• Do you think David wanted to be anointed king of Israel? Why or why not?

Say: The Bible reminds us that God looks at our hearts, not our outward appearance. Are there things in your heart that you don't want God to see? How will people know what's inside your heart and not just focus on the outside?

Slinger

(David Defeats Goliath)

1 Samuel 17:1-50

Energy Level

Medium Energy

This game will help your kids discover that David's killing Goliath was harder than it seemed. He was only successful because of God's help.

Supply List

❑ one long sock for every four students

❑ one ball for each sock (such as tennis balls or handballs)

❑ large area indoors or outdoors

❑ a bucket

The Game

Before the students arrive, place each ball in the toe of a sock. Explain to the students that the sling was an ancient weapon that was twirled around the head and then "slung" at a target. Say: **Today we are going to use these socks and test our "slinging" accuracy.**

Have the students line up at one end of your meeting space, and place the bucket at the other end. Let them take turns slinging the socks at the bucket for accuracy. Only after all the socks have been slung may children go to retrieve them. Make sure every student gets at least one turn.

Post-Game Discussion Questions

After the game, have the children sit down in groups of three and discuss these questions:

• **How hard did you find it to be accurate with your sling? Why?**

• **Do you think that being accurate with a real sling would be easier or harder? Why?**

• **If you had to face an angry giant, would you want to take only a sling? Why or why not?**

Say: **Slinging a ball at a target may be fun, but trying to hit a nine-foot target that is aiming at you is much scarier. God was with David and gave him victory over Goliath.**

Field of Protection

(Jonathan and David's Friendship)

1 Samuel 18:1-4; 19:1-7; 20:1-42

Energy Level

High Energy

This game will help your kids learn that God used David's best friend, Jonathan, to protect David from Saul.

Supply List

☐ none needed

The Game

Choose three volunteers—one to be David, one to be Jonathan, and one to be Saul. Have the rest of the group be the field boundaries by forming a circle around "David," standing about a foot apart, facing outward, and holding hands tightly. "Jonathan" and "Saul" should be on the outside of the circle.

Say: **Once there was a powerful king named Saul who was jealous of a boy named David.** Point to your Saul and David volunteers. **God favored David, because he had a pure heart and was right with God, which is why Saul was jealous of him. But Saul's son Jonathan was David's best friend.** Point to your Jonathan volunteer. **When David learned that Saul was trying to get him, David hid in a field, and Jonathan protected him from King Saul.**

Explain that when you tell them to go, Saul is going to try to crawl under the hands of the kids in the circle to tag David. But Jonathan is going to try to tag Saul. David needs to try to stay away from Saul inside the circle, but he can't leave the circle. Tell the kids in the circle to hold on tightly so Saul can't get to David.

The goal of the game is to protect David as much as possible. When someone gets tagged, find new volunteers for each part, and play the game again. Try to play enough times so each person has a turn to be David, Jonathan, or Saul.

Post-Game Discussion Questions

After playing this game, ask your students to sit in the groups they played the game with so there will be a David, a Jonathan, and a Saul in each group. Have them discuss these questions in their groups:

• **What was it like to protect David during this game? Why?**

• **How did God protect David from Saul in real life?**

• **How does God protect us in our lives?**

Say: **God protected David from Saul because God had a special plan for David. God can protect us, too, because he has a special plan for our lives as well.**

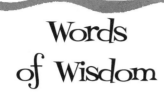

Words of Wisdom

(Solomon Asks for Wisdom)

1 Kings 2:1-4; 3:3-28

Energy Level

Low Energy

As your students learn about King Solomon, they'll appreciate the wisdom of God—and their parents!

Supply List

☐ none needed

The Game

Warmly greet your students, and say: **Let's play a game that will help us get to know each other.** Guide your kids as they form groups of two to four. **I want you to introduce yourself to your group. Tell the group your name plus something wise you've learned from your parents.** Give them examples such as, "I'm Mrs. Black, and my mother told me to always turn off the hot water first when I finish filling the bathtub."

Please listen carefully, because you'll need to remember your friends' names *and* the wisdom they shared. Explain that all the groups will come back together and introduce their group members to the whole class.

When the class comes back together, give an example of an introduction such as, "This is my friend John. His father told him not to skate around parked cars." Help students determine the order of introductions by suggesting that whoever is wearing the most red give the first introduction. Continue until everyone has been introduced.

Post-Game Discussion Questions

After playing this game, debrief with the entire group using these questions as a guide:

• **What have you learned from others in the group?**

• **Who do you ask when you need wisdom?**

• **Why did Solomon ask God for wisdom?**

Say: **People are always looking for the best way to handle a problem or circumstance. Everyone needs wisdom. Solomon asked God for wisdom, and so can we.**

Oil Jars and Sticks Grab

(Elijah Helps a Widow)

1 Kings 17:7-24

Energy Level

Medium Energy

Children will gather pretend sticks and oil jars to simulate what the widow was doing when Elijah began to interact with her.

Supply List

❑ small wooden sticks or stick-like objects (such as Tinkertoys, capped markers, new unsharpened pencils, or craft sticks), three per child

❑ small paper cups, one per child

❑ clean cloth blindfolds (optional)

The Game

Scatter the "sticks" and "oil jars" over half the play area. Two or more children at a time will be blindfolded or keep their eyes closed as they take turns crawling to the sticks and oil jars. Each child should collect at least one oil jar and two or three sticks, then open his or her eyes and walk or trot back to the group. As each child returns to the group, another child crawls away to gather sticks and a jar. Coach those at the starting line to give verbal suggestions and encouragement as others "hunt" and to cheer when someone returns with "the goods." When the last children return to the starting line, celebrate with whoops and cheers.

Post-Game Discussion Questions

After finishing the game, have everyone sit down and discuss the game using these questions:

• How did you feel trying to blindly find the sticks and oil jars? Why?

• Did you feel any differently once you found what you were searching for? Explain.

• Elijah helped the widow, through God's power, by giving her what she needed. How did the other players' cheering and encouragement help you while you played the game?

Say: Sometimes we can't see what God has in store for us, just as you couldn't see what you were looking for. But like God used Elijah to help the widow, God helps us, too, when we have a need.

Will You Buy an Idol?

(Elijah and the Prophets of Baal)

1 Kings 18:16-40
Energy Level
Low Energy

This game will help your kids realize the powerlessness of idols as they review the story of Elijah and the prophets of Baal.

Supply List
☐ none needed

The Game

Have children sit in a circle. Ask two volunteers to go to the center of the circle; they'll be the Idol-Seller and the Idol. Say: **After Elijah's showdown with the prophets of Baal on Mount Carmel, there may have been a lot of people wanting to get rid of their Baal idols.**

The Idol-Seller will try to sell his or her Idol to the children in the circle. The Idol-Seller will choose one person and ask, "Will you buy an idol?" That player must answer, "No, thank you," with a straight face. Then the seller will say, "My Idol can do cool things like...Will you buy an idol now?"

The child playing the part of the idol will try to do whatever the seller says it can do, such as tap dance, sing a song, do a somersault, and so on. Then the player in the circle must answer, "No, thank you," again with a straight face. If the player cracks a smile or laughs, he or she becomes the new Idol, the Idol becomes the Idol-Seller, and the Idol-Seller joins the circle. Play until all the children have had a turn to be either the Idol or the Idol-Seller.

Post-Game Discussion Questions

After playing this game, ask your students to sit down in groups of three and discuss:

• **What was the goofiest thing you just saw someone ask an idol to do?**

• **What goofy thing did the prophets of Baal ask their idol to do? Were they successful? Could Baal do** *anything***?**

• **How did Elijah show everyone who was boss?**

Say: **The prophets of Baal were defeated in a big way when their false god couldn't light the sacrifice on fire. But the real, true God ignited not only Elijah's sacrifice, but even the altar and all the water around it! It's ridiculous to trust something or someone other than the one true God. He's the one with the** *real* **power.**

Overflowing Oil

(Elisha Helps a Widow)

2 Kings 4:1-7

Energy Level

High Energy

Children will experience the excitement of trying to gather all the "oil" that's being supplied, just like widow did when God used Elisha to bless her with an abundance of oil.

Supply List

❑ garbage bags or paper or plastic grocery bags, one per three to four kids

❑ lots of wadded newspaper or scrap paper

❑ clock or watch with a second hand, or a timer

❑ an adult helper or two

The Game

Kids will try to collect as much "oil" in the form of paper wads in a short span of time (up to one minute). Divide kids into groups of three or four, and give each group one bag. Toss wadded paper all over the room. Tell students they'll have one minute (or less time, if you choose) to collect as much "oil" (paper wads) as they can. Shout "go" and start timing. As the groups collect, have adult helpers toss out more wadded paper, so there's always more to be collected. When time's up, shout "stop." Have players give others in their group and everyone else high fives, congratulations, and positive words for their hard work.

Post-Game Discussion Questions

When the game is over, gather everyone for a discussion, using these questions as prompts:

• **What was it like trying to fill up your "oil jar" (your bag) before time was up? Why?**

• **How did you feel when you were done and had a big bag full of "oil"?**

• **In what ways would you like God to bless you and your family?**

Say: **When we tell God about what we need, we can trust him to provide it. Sometimes God gives us even more than we expect!**

Healing Naaman
(God Heals Naaman)

2 Kings 5:1-16
Energy Level
Medium Energy
This game will help your kids experience how God cared for Naaman.

Supply List
☐ one adhesive bandage for each child

The Game

Choose one child to be Naaman. Number off the rest of the children from one to seven, repeating as necessary until every child has a number. Have "Naaman" stand at one end of the room and the rest of the class stand at the opposite end. Place a pile of adhesive bandages next to Naaman.

Call off a number from one to seven in random order. Every child with that number will run to Naaman, open a bandage, and place it somewhere on Naaman—but *not* on his face. When all seven numbers have been called off and all the children have had a turn to place a bandage on Naaman, have Naaman dip himself up and down seven times as the class counts out loud. Then call off the numbers again in random order and have the children with each number run to Naaman and remove a bandage until he is completely "healed" and all the children have had a turn.

Post-Game Discussion Questions

After playing this game, ask your students to sit down in groups of three and discuss:

• **How do you think Naaman felt when he had to dip himself up and down seven times in the muddy river? Why?**

• **Why do you think that God chose this way to heal Naaman?**

• **Can you tell about a time that you asked God to make you feel better?**

Close in prayer, thanking God for caring about all of our needs.

Praise Songs

(Jehoshaphat Trusts God)

2 Chronicles 20:1-30
Energy Level
Medium Energy
In this game your kids will think of
songs that contain the word *praise*
as they relate to Jehoshaphat
praising God in the face of attack.

Supply List
❏ none needed

The Game

Help the children form
groups of two to six,
depending on the total
size of your group. Say: **When
Jehoshaphat, the king of Judah, faced
attack from an enemy army, he asked
God what to do. Then, as he followed
God's instructions, the people sang
praises to God all the way to meet
their enemies.**

Explain that in this game, each
group will need to think of songs that
contain the word *praise* in either the
title or the lyrics. Every time they think
of a song, they should stand up and
start singing it, or at least the portion
that contains the word *praise*. If

another group is singing, they must
wait until that group finishes before
singing their own song. Challenge kids
to come up with as many different
"praise" songs as they can. Continue
until each group has sung at least one
(or two or three) song portion(s). You
may want to make a list yourself
beforehand, in case kids need help
getting started.

Post-Game Discussion Questions

After playing this game, have students sit down in their groups and
discuss:

• **What made this game hard? What
made it easy?**

• **What made Jehoshaphat's job difficult? How did God make it easy?**

• **How do you think you would
have felt if you were in Jehoshaphat's
army, singing praise songs as you
marched out to meet your enemies?
Explain.**

• **How would you have felt to see
that God really did fight the battle for
you? Explain.**

Say: **When Jehoshaphat faced a
scary, dangerous situation, he asked
God what to do about it. And God
saved the whole land of Judah! God
wants us to talk with him too when we
face scary situations. God is there to
help us when we trust in him.**

Temple Treasure Hunt

(Josiah Discovers God's Word)

2 Chronicles 34:1-33

Energy Level

Medium Energy

This game gives your students an opportunity to use teamwork as they explore the story of King Josiah cleaning the Lord's Temple.

Supply List

❑ Bibles, one per three or four children

❑ coins or toy money, at least one piece per three children

❑ toy blocks, at least one per three children

❑ safe, new cleaning supplies (such as a dust cloth, sponge, whisk broom, or pictures of these), one per three or four children

❑ grocery bags, one per three or four children

The Game

Before the game, hide the temple treasures (the supplies, minus the grocery bags) around your playing area. Be sure to hide at least one treasure for each player. If you have time and sup-plies handy, you might hide two or three treasures for each player to find.

Bring the kids to your playing area. Say: **When King Josiah told his workers to clean up and rebuild the Lord's Temple, it probably felt like a treasure hunt. There were lots of closets and shelves, nooks and crannies, and fallen-down rooms to hunt through and clean up. We're going to get into teams and work together to find all the temple treasures that are hidden here.**

Briefly review what was found in the Temple or used to fix it up: God's Word, money, cleaning supplies, and building materials. Tell the kids that they will look for Bibles, coins, cleaning supplies, and blocks (or whichever specific supplies you chose).

Divide the kids into teams of three or four, and give each team a bag to keep their treasures in. At your signal, kids may separate and start looking in the designated area for the temple treasures. Whenever anyone finds a treasure, he or she brings it to his or her team's bag. If you hid more than one treasure per child, tell the kids how many items each may look for (to make sure everyone gets a turn to find some-thing). If one team finishes early, they may give hints to the other teams about where they saw more treasure hidden.

When all the temple treasures have been found, gather the teams back together with their bags. Let the teams briefly show the other teams what treasures they found. Congratu-late the kids for being good workers in the "temple."

Post-Game Discussion Questions

After playing this game, ask your students to sit down in their groups and discuss:

• How do you think the Temple workers felt about fixing up the Temple after it hadn't been used in many years? Explain your answer.

• Why should we take care of our place of worship?

• What can kids do to help take care of our church?

Say: Let's pray and thank God for giving us a special place where we can worship him.

Nehemiah's Super-Sneaky Inspection

(Nehemiah Rebuilds the Wall)

Nehemiah 2:11–6:19

Energy Level

Medium Energy
This game will remind children how Nehemiah started the God-given task of rebuilding Jerusalem's walls by sneaking in at night to inspect the situation.

Supply List

❑ clean blindfolds, one for every two kids

❑ blocks, such as preschool building blocks, Duplo plastic preschool toys, empty boxes, and so on

The Game

This game re-creates Nehemiah's silent nighttime inspection of Jerusalem. Have half the children put on blindfolds (or agree to keep their eyes closed) and randomly lay on the floor in the play area. Scatter the blocks around the "sleeping people of Jerusalem." Turn out the lights if you desire.

The other kids will attempt to sneak around the room, tiptoeing around and over the Sleepers, collecting the blocks. If a Sleeper hears someone, the Sleeper can reach out a hand to try to tag him or her. If tagged, the Sneaker lies down and becomes a Sleeper. Play for a set amount of time (two to three minutes) or until the blocks are collected. Then have Sleepers and Sneakers switch places and play again.

Post-Game Discussion Questions

After the game is over, have children talk about the game using these questions as discussion prompts:

• Which was harder—sneaking or sleeping? Why?

• How did God show his favor to Nehemiah in this late-night sneaky inspection?

• What kinds of things could God ask of you that are hard jobs, like Nehemiah's work of rebuilding Jerusalem's walls?

Say: Nehemiah used his smarts and God's wisdom to get a big job done God's way. Remember that the next time you have a big job to do!

Test of Courage Game

(Queen Esther Is Brave)

Esther 2:1-18; 4:1–5:8; 7:1–8:17

Energy Level

Low Energy

This game will give kids an opportunity to test their courage and increase their understanding of the courage Queen Esther showed.

Supply List

❑ several dozen raw eggs

❑ box of saltine crackers (keep hidden)

❑ sections of newspaper to use as a dropcloth

❑ adult accomplice to help you

❑ blindfold (very important!)

The Game

Explain that this game will test each person's courage as he or she walks the Courage Corridor. Keep the crackers hidden as you show the children the eggs, and together place sections of newsprint on the floor in a hallway or corridor. Ask for several of the children to accompany your accomplice to another room where they can't hear or see what you're doing.

Once your small group has left, enlist children's help in picking up the eggs and returning them to cartons. Ask children to replace the eggs with many stacks of three or four saltines. Explain that when someone wearing shoes steps on the saltines, expecting eggs, it will sound like eggs breaking.

Ask your accomplice to securely blindfold one child and bring him or her out to walk the Courage Corridor. The goal: Get to the end of the corridor without breaking an egg.

As the child steps on crackers—imagining a raw egg—lead the children in saying things like, "Gross!" and "Yuck!"

At the end of the corridor, applaud the walker's courage and remove the blindfold. Repeat the process with each child who was removed from the room.

Post-Game Discussion Questions

After the game, ask students to sit down and discuss the experience. Start the discussion with these questions:

• What did you feel like as you waited for your courage to be tested? Explain.

• How did other people's reactions and sounds affect your courage?

• How did it feel to watch someone doing something brave?

• What's something brave and bold you've done that didn't involve eggs and crackers?

Say: **Queen Esther didn't know what her boldness would bring. God rewarded her courage. When you're brave like Queen Esther, God will be faithful to help you go ahead even if you're feeling scared.**

Matching From Memory

(Esther Saves Her People)

Esther 8:17; 9:18-23

Energy Level

Low Energy

This game will help your kids discover that God wants them to honor him as together you explore how Esther was honored for saving her people.

Supply List

❑ index cards, four per student

❑ crayons or markers, one per student

❑ newsprint with the dates of Easter and Thanksgiving written on it

The Game

Help students form groups of three. Pass out twelve index cards and three crayons or markers to each group. Have each person write his or her name on one index card. Then have students each write his or her birth date on another card. After everyone finishes, each group should still have six blank cards left.

Ask each group to write these holiday names, one holiday per card: Easter, Thanksgiving, and Christmas. On their last three cards, have them write the dates those holidays are celebrated. Direct kids' attention to the newsprint you've posted with the dates, in case they need some help. When finished, have each group put all their cards together and mix them up.

Say: **You're going to play a game with your group that you might know as Concentration or Memory.** Have each group lay all their cards face down in three rows of four cards each. Have students take turns at turning up two cards and seeing if they match. If they don't, then they'll turn them both over and the next student takes a turn. Encourage them to pay attention to what others turn over and try to remember the location so that when it's their turn they'll have a better chance at getting a match. When a student makes a match, he or she may set the matching cards aside and give someone else a turn.

Post-Game Discussion Questions

After playing this game, ask your students to sit down with their groups and discuss:

• How does it feel when someone remembers your birthday?

• Why should we remember the good things God has done for us?

• What's one thing God has done for you that you want to remember?

Say: Jewish people celebrate Purim every year to remember how Esther helped them. It's important for them to celebrate and remember, and it's important that we remember the good things God has done too.

When we're sad or discouraged, we can think about times when God has helped us and remember that he's promised to always be with us.

Herding the Sheep

(The Lord Is My Shepherd)

Psalm 23
Energy Level
High Energy

This game reminds children that Jesus is our shepherd. He loves us all and wants all of us safely in his care.

Supply List
☐ none needed

The Game

Gather children together in a large open area to explain the game. Say: **God is like a shepherd who works hard to keep all of his sheep safe and close to him. We're going to play a game to see how the shepherd herds his sheep.**

Choose one child or adult helper to be the shepherd. Divide the remaining children into two groups of approximately equal size. Have the groups line up on opposite sides of the playing area. Place the Shepherd in the middle of the playing area. The Shepherd will call for the Sheep by yelling "Come, Sheep." The Sheep will try to run to the other side of the playing area without being caught by the Shepherd. Both sides will run simultaneously so that the two groups change sides. The Shepherd will try to tag the sheep as they run by.

Any children who are tagged by the Shepherd will become part of the herd. The Shepherd will call for the Sheep again, but this time the children who were caught will help the Shepherd tag the others. Remind the children to be careful not to run into each other. Play will continue until all the Sheep have been tagged and the herd has been restored.

To keep this game from becoming a competition, be sure to emphasize that the goal is to restore the herd.

Post-Game Discussion Questions

As children rest after playing the game, lead them in the following discussion:

• **How is God like a shepherd?**

• **Like the shepherd in this game, God never gives up on us. How does it feel to know that God will always love and protect you no matter what you do?**

• **Do you think God sometimes feels like we are running away from him? How do you think that makes him feel?**

Say: **How exciting to know that God loves us and cares for us like a shepherd cares for his sheep!**

Burning-Coal Bustle

(Isaiah Sees God's Holiness)

Isaiah 6:1-8
Energy Level
Medium Energy

This game brings to mind the way seraphs carried a burning coal in tongs in Isaiah's vision of God.

Supply List
❑ kitchen tongs, one set per three to six kids

❑ small cube-shaped items such as dice, blocks, and so on, two to four per player

❑ empty box, such as a shoe box

The Game

Explain that students will carry blocks with tongs the same way a seraph carried a burning coal to purify Isaiah when he saw the Lord. Scatter blocks (or dice) at one end of the play area. Have kids stand behind the blocks. At the other end of the room place an empty box. Hand out the kitchen tongs. At your signal, whoever has tongs will use them to pick up a block. Then they will walk on tiptoe to the box and drop the block into the box.

Next, the children duck walk back to the starting area, jump up, and shout, "Here am I! Send me!" (Isaiah's words). Then they pass the tongs to another player. Continue until all the blocks are in the box.

Post-Game Discussion Questions

When the game is over, ask children to sit down in groups of three and discuss:

• **Why did the seraph carry a burning coal to Isaiah and touch his lips?**

• **How would you have felt if you had seen God like Isaiah did? Explain.**

• **How do we get cleaned from our sins today?**

Say: **Isaiah was able to volunteer to do God's work because he knew he needed forgiveness from sin and he admitted it to God. God is just as available to us when we need to ask for forgiveness for our sins.**

Lion. Lion. Shut Your Mouth!

(Daniel Is Safe in the Lions' Den)

Daniel 6:1-23
Energy Level

Medium Energy

This game will help students review the story of Daniel in the lions' den and its lesson of courage in standing up for one's convictions.

Supply List
☐ none needed

The Game

Ask for two volunteers, one to be the angel of the Lord who shuts the lions' mouths and the other to be Daniel. All other students can be lions.

Place "Daniel" and the "angel" at one end of the room, and line up the "lions" at the other end. The lions must crawl on their knees toward Daniel. Encourage them to growl, roar, and paw the air like real lions as they advance toward Daniel. As the closest lion nears Daniel (and just before the lion touches Daniel), the person playing the angel should shout loudly: "Lion, Lion, shut your mouth!" All the lions must crawl as quickly as possible back to the other end of the room and start over.

To demonstrate, you might be the first angel. Have students take turns playing Daniel and the angel. Play until everyone has had a turn to be either Daniel or the angel, or as time allows.

Post-Game Discussion Questions

After playing the game, ask children to sit down in groups of three and discuss:

• **What was the "funnest" part to play in this game? Why?**

• **How did it feel to be the angel who got to tell the lions to shut their mouths? Why?**

• **Have you ever gotten in trouble for doing something that was right to do? What happened, and how did you feel?**

• **Did you ever try to do what was right even though you knew you might get teased for it? How did you feel about that? What did you end up doing?**

The story of Daniel is a classic account of one man who took a stand for God. Today's students can enjoy the story and be encouraged to do the same.

Trust Trash

(Jonah Learns to Obey God)

Jonah 1:1–4:11

Energy Level

High Energy

This game will help your kids discover why trusting God is important through the story of Jonah and the big fish.

Supply List

❑ one blanket for every four or five students

❑ one action figure or doll for every four or five students

❑ one large, empty trash can

The Game

Help children form groups of four or five students. Pass out a folded blanket and an action figure or doll to each group. Have groups spread out around the meeting area, and place the trash can in the center somewhere so that all groups have an unobstructed view. Each group should be at least six to eight feet away from the trash can.

Ask groups to imagine that their blanket is the sea, their action figure or doll is Jonah, and the trash can is the mouth of the big fish. Groups must use their blankets to get Jonah into the trash can, without walking over to it.

One by one, have groups try to launch their action figure or doll into the trash can using blankets (this will probably work best if the blanket is folded once so it's not so big). Have groups take as many turns as time allows. Remind students to watch out and be careful as the dolls go flying toward the trash can, and to try to avoid hitting another person with the flying dolls.

When time is up, congratulate all groups on a job well done.

Post-Game Discussion Questions

After playing this game, ask your students to sit down in their groups and discuss:

• Why did God put Jonah in the belly of the big fish?

• If it had been you being thrown into the belly of the fish, what would you have felt? Why?

• Why is it hard to trust God sometimes?

• Why should we obey God even when we're afraid of what he's asking?

Say: Jonah didn't want to obey God, but after he spent three nights in the belly of the whale, he realized that God's way is always best. God wants us to know that obeying him is always right, even when we are afraid, because he will be there for us.

Manger Mania

(Jesus Is Born)

Luke 1:26-38; 2:1-20

Energy Level

High Energy

Your kids will learn about Jesus' birth through the eyes of the shepherds as they play this active tag game.

Supply List

❑ twelve pieces of old cloth or crumpled paper, each with one verse of Luke 2:8-19 written on it

❑ six to eight plastic cones or other visible boundary markers (optional)

The Game

You will need a fairly large, open space to play this game. If you don't have a large space available, then play the game with kids moving around on their seats instead of running. Mark off the four corners of the play area, plus the centerline. On one end of the playing area, place the cloths that have Luke 2:8-13 on them. On the other end of the play area, place the cloths with Luke 2:14-19 on them.

Form your children into two teams of equal number. One team will be designated as the Shepherds, and the other team will be the Sheep. Send the two teams to opposite sides of the play area.

The object of the game is to reach the end of the opposing team's playing area, retrieve all the pieces of cloth from "the manger," and place the cloths in sequential order. Kids may retrieve only one cloth at a time. When a player crosses the middle line into the other team's playing area, the opposing team members can tag the person before he or she reaches the manger. If that happens, the child must return back across the centerline and begin again. If a player obtains a cloth from the opposing side, he or she is free to walk back to the other side of the playing area without losing the cloth.

Once a team has obtained all the verse cloths from the opposing team's manger, they gather together, attempt to put them in sequential order as found in Luke 2, and read the passage first to the leader and then to the whole group. (Note that early readers may need help in sequencing the verse cloths.) Continue the game until both teams have obtained their six cloths.

Post-Game Discussion Questions

After playing this game, ask your students to sit down as a large group and discuss:

• How do you think the shepherds felt when the angel of the Lord appeared to them in the field? Why?

• Why do you think God chose to reveal this information to the shepherds instead of some other people?

• Luke 2:19 says, "But Mary treasured up all these things and pondered them in her heart." Why do you think she treasured them? What would you have been thinking about if you were Mary?

Say: We can see through our fun look at Luke 2 that God had a special plan for the shepherds in the field the night Jesus was born; they were the first to see Jesus and then tell others about him.

Finding Flavor
(Wise Men Find Jesus)

Matthew 2:1-12
Energy Level

Medium Energy

This game will help students identify how we pursue things that are important to us.

Supply List

❑ one small bag of healthy snack items (such as baby carrots or crackers) per two to three students

The Game

Before class, make up several small bags of healthy treats, so that you have one bag per two to three children. Make up one bag of each kind of treat (one bag of carrots, one bag of cereal snack mix, one bag of crackers, and so on). You may want to prepare one or two extra bags to allow for visitors. Before children arrive, hide the treat bags around the classroom. Make sure they are not in plain sight. But remember where you hid them!

Explain to students they'll play a scavenger hunt game called "Finding Flavor." Divide students into groups of two or three, and assign a treat type to each group. Each group will work together to find its assigned treat. Tell the waiting groups to watch carefully, as they probably will get clues to where their own treats are hidden!

Tell kids that you will be their guide and give them the "getting hotter" and "getting colder" clues, with "hot" indicating that the students are getting closer to the hidden item. Direct the first group in this manner to find the first bag of treats. When one group has finished, let the next group take its turn. Repeat until all groups have had a turn to find a treat bag. You may either let each group eat its treats as they find them, or have children wait until all the groups have found a treat. (Either way you are likely to have a grumbler or two, but you know your kids and what works best for them.)

Note: If you have less class time and more helpers available, you could have one adult leader assigned to each group giving the "hot" and "cold" clues and have all the groups hunt at the same time.

Post-Game Discussion Questions

When everyone has finished, bring the groups back together and mix them up into new groups to discuss the following questions:

• What kept you searching for the treat bag?

• Have you ever lost something important to you? What did you do?

• How do you go about looking for important things you want to find? Who do you turn to for help to find them?

• How did the leader help you find your treats in this game?

• How is that like how God helped the wise men find Jesus?

Say: **The wise men were sort of like us in our scavenger hunt. They kept looking for Jesus, even though it took a long time, because it was so important to them to find him. And they relied on God's help, through the star, to guide them.**

Change Charades

(Jesus Grows Up)

Luke 2:39-52

Energy Level

Medium Energy

This game will help your kids identify positive behaviors that will help them grow up just like Jesus.

Supply List

❏ a large sheet of poster board

❏ a marker

❏ masking tape

❏ a beanbag

❏ Bible

The Game

Use a marker to divide the poster board into four squares. Write one of these categories in each square: "Wisdom," "Physically," "Friendship With God," and "Friendship With People." Place the poster on the floor. Tape a masking tape line on the floor about six feet away from the poster.

Read Luke 2:52 to the children in an age-appropriate translation. Say: **Jesus was a child just like you. He had to grow up and mature into an adult— just like you. Let's play a game that will help us think about the things we can do to grow up healthy like Jesus did!**

Explain to the children that they will take turns standing on the tape line and tossing the beanbag at the poster. Each child will look at what square he or she hit with the beanbag and act out one thing they can do to grow in this area. For example, if a child hits the "Friendship With People" square, he or she might act out a scene in which a child shares a toy. Allow the children to grab a partner if they would like one. But remind them that they cannot talk when they act out their scene. Ask other children to try to guess what it is that they are acting out. Continue until every child has had at least one turn to toss the beanbag and act out something.

Post-Game Discussion Questions

After each child has had a turn to lead a charade, ask:

• Why was it important for Jesus to grow in these four areas?

• How can Jesus help you as you grow in these four areas?

• What is one area that you can ask Jesus to help you grow in this week?

Say: **Jesus is an example for all kids as they grow up. By paying attention to strengthening your body, your mind, your friendships with people, and your friendship with God, you can grow up just like Jesus did! This will help you get ready for a whole lifetime of pleasing God.**

Shoe-Tie Guy

(John Baptizes Jesus)

Mark 1:4-11

Energy Level

High Energy
Kids will play a high-octane game to discover what it means to serve Jesus.

Supply List

☐ a game die

The Game

Say: **John the Baptist said he wasn't important enough to untie Jesus' sandals. Let's play a game to help us understand what John meant by this.**

Ask for a volunteer to roll the die as the rest of the kids walk around. Have the child roll the die and call out the number rolled. When a number is called, the children will form groups of that many children. In each group, the children will form a group and stand so everyone in the group has one foot touching someone else's foot in the group.

After the number is called, call out one of these ways toes can touch: toe-to-toe, heel-to-toe, or heel-to-heel. Make up more ways if you'd like!

Children who didn't manage to join a group of the correct number will join in a group with an adult.

Alternate the person rolling the die every four roles.

Post-Game Discussion Questions

After playing this game, ask your students to sit down as a large group and discuss:

• Which was the hardest way to touch feet? the easiest?

• Why do you think John said he wasn't good enough to untie Jesus' shoes?

• What attitude should we have as we serve Jesus?

Say: **The truth is, it's a privilege to serve Jesus. John the Baptist knew that it was an** *honor* **to be allowed to serve Jesus. Jesus honors us, too, when he tells us that he wants us to serve him. We can serve Jesus with a great attitude knowing that we have the best job in the whole world.**

Temptation Obstacle Course

(Satan Tempts Jesus)

Luke 4:1-13; Matthew 4:1-11

Energy Level

Medium Energy

This game will help your kids actively review how Satan tempted Jesus and how the angels took care of Jesus.

Supply List

❑ one large pan of sand
❑ one medium-sized rock that the children can easily carry
❑ one small step stool
❑ one table
❑ one adhesive bandage for each child

The Game

Set up the obstacle course as described in your instructions, and have the children watch you walk through the obstacle course before they try it themselves. As you go through each stage, explain the part of the story that stage represents.

Say: **First, you'll walk through this** pan of sand, just as Jesus walked through the desert. Next, you'll pick up the stone, like the one Satan tried to get Jesus to turn into bread. Carry it around this circle, and put it back where you found it.

Then, bend down and crawl under the table, to remind you that Satan tried to get Jesus to bend down and worship him. Next, stand on the step stool and jump off, to remind you that Satan tried to get Jesus to jump off the highest point of the Temple. Finally, unwrap a bandage and place it on yourself, to remind you that the angels came and cared for Jesus after he was tempted.

Have children go through the obstacle course, resetting it for each child as needed.

Post-Game Discussion Questions

After playing this game, ask your students to sit down in groups of three and discuss:

• How does it feel to know that even though Satan tempted Jesus, Jesus never gave in? Why?

• What is one way that Satan tempts you?

• What can you do to resist Satan's temptations?

Close in prayer, asking God to help each child resist temptations during the coming week.

Water Into Wine

(Jesus' First Miracle)

John 2:1-11

Energy Level

Medium Energy
This game will help your kids discover the wonder of Jesus' first miracle.

Supply List

❑ two packages of non-sweetened purple drink mix for each group of ten
❑ two large pots for each group of ten
❑ one cup for each group of ten
❑ one large stirring spoon for each group of ten
❑ water

The Game

After you've warmly greeted your class, form the children into groups of ten or less and have them stand with their groups at one end of the room. If you have fewer than ten children, keep them all together. At the other end of the room, set up the following items so that each group has its own supplies: one large pot with two packages of drink mix dumped out in the bottom, one large pot of water, one cup, and one large stirring spoon.

Say: **I want you to work as a team to change the water in this pot into "wine" in that pot.** Point to each appropriate pot as you speak. **Each of you will go and scoop out one cup of water and pour it into the other pot, then go back to your group. When everyone has poured one cup of water into the pot, each of you should take a turn going down and stirring the pot with the spoon.** Have the last child from each group scoop out a cup of "wine" from the pot to show how they turned plain water into "wine."

Post-Game Discussion Questions

After playing this game, ask your students to sit down in groups of three and discuss:

• **Did you really turn water into wine during the game? Could you?**

• **Do you think Jesus had to work as hard as you just did to change the water into wine? Why or why not?**

Say: **We had fun changing our water into "wine" today, but we were just pretending. Jesus really changed the water into wine. Jesus could do that because he is the Son of God.**

Following Jesus

(Disciples Follow Jesus)

Mark 1:14-20

Energy Level

Medium Energy
This game will help children understand that their actions can let others know they are followers of Jesus.

Supply List

❑ none needed

The Game

Have the children stand in a circle. Say: **The disciples didn't just follow Jesus around, they learned to care about what he cared about, and to behave like Jesus behaved.**

In this game, one of you will play the part of Jesus. The rest of us will be disciples. If "Jesus" claps his hands, we'll all clap our hands. If "Jesus" pats his head, we'll all pat our heads. Sounds easy, right? Let children respond. **The hard part is, one of you will be an outsider and won't know who "Jesus" is. You'll have to watch the group and guess which player is "Jesus."**

Send a volunteer briefly outside the room. Then choose one child to be "Jesus." Bring the "outsider" back into the room and into the middle of the circle. "Jesus" should begin making hand motions that everyone else follows. Some examples of hand motions or actions include reaching for the sky, waving hands in the air, touching toes, and so on. Children will stay in a circle and copy the actions of "Jesus." The "outsider" will observe from the center of the circle and try to determine which child is "Jesus."

The "outsider" will have three turns to guess which child is "Jesus." If all three guesses are incorrect, the adult leader will reveal the identity of "Jesus." After the identity of "Jesus" has been revealed, choose a new "outsider" and a new "Jesus." Continue playing until all children have had a turn to be either "Jesus" or the "outsider" or until children tire of the game.

Post-Game Discussion Questions

After the game, lead children through the following discussion:

• How could you tell who everyone was following?

• How should we live and act to make sure that people know that we are followers of Jesus?

• How do you think Jesus feels when we say we are his followers and then treat others badly?

Say: **People should know by our words and actions that we are followers of Jesus.**

Kneezies

(Jesus Heals a Paralytic)

Mark 2:1-12

Energy Level

Medium Energy

This game will help children know how it feels to have restricted mobility and that Jesus cares for everyone's needs.

Supply List

❑ foam rubber or other soft balls, one per five or six children

The Game

Divide the children into teams of five or six. Have one child on each team put a soft ball between his or her knees. Instruct children to walk a designated distance and back again without dropping the ball. They can't use their hands to hold the ball in place. Remind children that this is *not* a race, just a different way of trying to get across the room. If they drop the ball, have them pick it up and put it back between their knees and continue.

As children do this, say: **It's harder to walk when you can't move your legs freely, isn't it? People who have hurt their legs or are born with crippled legs can't move their legs like most of you do.** When each child has had a turn, begin another relay by changing the instructions to hopping, running, or skipping with the ball between their knees.

Post-Game Discussion Questions

After playing this game, ask your students to sit down in groups of three and discuss:

• **What do you think it would feel like to not be able to run and play? Explain.**

• **How could you get from place to place if you couldn't walk?**

• **How do you think Jesus feels about our needs?**

Say: **It feels good to be able to run, doesn't it? The paralytic man couldn't even walk, but he had friends who cared about him so much that they took him to see Jesus. Jesus healed the man because he cared about him too. Jesus cares about everyone's needs.**

Sinking Sails

(Jesus Calms a Storm)

Mark 4:35-41

Energy Level

High Energy

This game will help children know God is in control, and help children know how the disciples felt while at sea in a storm.

Supply List

☐ masking tape
☐ lots of newspaper

The Game

Tape a simple outline of a boat on a large area of the floor. Crumple several sheets of newspaper and place them inside the boat. Place several crumpled pieces outside the boat also. Choose three or four children at a time to be disciples and stand inside the boat. Say: **The disciples were out on a lake when a storm blew in. They were afraid the wind would blow them overboard or that the boat would sink because water was filling it!**

Tell the children they are going to pretend the newspaper is water and they must bail (toss) it out of the boat. The children on the outside of the boat will be the storm and keep tossing paper back into the boat. Let them make soft "howling wind" sounds as they toss the paper. Remind the children inside the boat to stay within the boat, so they don't go overboard. Set a designated time to play, then switch "disciples" so that all the children get a turn to play inside the boat.

Post-Game Discussion Questions

After playing this game, ask your students to sit down in groups of three and discuss:

• **What did you do to keep your "boat" from "sinking"?**

• **How do you think you would feel if you were out in a real storm? Explain.**

• **What other kinds of trouble might you need Jesus' help with?**

Say: **The disciples were afraid their boat was sinking. They needed someone to help them. Jesus spoke to the sea and it became calm. We can call on Jesus when we are afraid and he will hear us. Jesus will calm our fears.**

Can You Do That Blindfolded?

(Jesus Heals the Blind Man)

Mark 10:46-52

Energy Level

Low Energy

This game will help your kids discover what it may be like to be blind.

Supply List

❏ one blindfold for each child in your class (you could use an old sheet ripped in strips, dish towels, bandannas, old neckties, scarves, or stocking caps pulled down over children's eyes)

❏ one piece of paper for each child

❏ one pencil for each child

❏ one box of crayons

❏ one soft foam ball

The Game

Say: **Today we'll find out what it might be like to be blind. I'm going to ask you to try several different things while you are blindfolded.** Help the children put on their blindfolds. After each challenge, give children a few minutes to attempt what you have asked them to do. Use these challenges:

• **Try to tie or buckle your shoes.**

• **Using the paper and pencil in front of you, draw a happy face and then write your name under it.**

• **Pass around a box of crayons. When you receive the box, choose the color I ask you for.**

• **When I call your name, I'll toss you a soft ball. Try to catch it.**

• **Someone will stand in front of you. When I call your name, tell me who is in front of you without touching the person or talking to him or her.**

Post-Game Discussion Questions

After playing this game, help the children remove their blindfolds. Ask your students to sit down in groups of three and discuss:

• **How did it feel to try to do those things when you couldn't see? Explain.**

• **What do you think would be most challenging about being blind?**

• **How do you think the man in the Bible story felt when Jesus healed him?**

Have the children join you in a large circle after the discussion time.

Say: **We're going to say a one-word** prayer of thanks to God. I'll begin our prayer time; each of you (starting with the child on your left) **will then get a turn telling God one thing that you're thankful for that you can see. When everyone has had a turn, I'll close our prayer time.**

Note: Be sensitive to the realities of your children's lives. If you have a child who's blind, or whose life is touched by vision impairment, consider not playing this game, or playing it and asking that child how the experience is or isn't like what the child experiences.

Feeding Frenzy

(Jesus Feeds Five Thousand)

John 6:1-15

Energy Level

High Energy

As your students explore the story of Jesus feeding the five thousand, your kids will discover how God provides for them, too.

Supply List

❑ one shallow, rectangular laundry basket (not the tall, vertical kind)

❑ one carton of goldfish crackers

❑ one loaf of sweet bread, or a bag of bagels or rolls

❑ furniture or objects in your meeting area

❑ masking tape

❑ paper towels or napkins

The Game

Arrange furniture or other objects in your meeting area to create a simple obstacle course. Students will maneuver through the course while balancing a laundry basket on their heads, so set it up with this in mind. Include things for them to safely step over, move around, or get past. Create arrows on the floor with masking tape to show the direction of the course.

Help the children divide into groups of four. Point out the starting point of the obstacle course and the laundry basket containing the carton of goldfish crackers and the bag or loaf of bread. Explain that each group will get a turn to balance the laundry basket on their heads (no hands allowed!) and move together through the obstacle course to the other end (with the basket of food still on their heads!). Have groups do the course one at a time, while the others cheer them on from the sidelines.

Post-Game Discussion Questions

After playing this game, pass out paper towels and some of the crackers and bread to your students, and ask them to discuss these questions in their groups:

• **What was easy about this game? What was hard about it?**

• **In the Bible story, how did Jesus show all those people that God cared for them?**

• **How has God taken care of other people that you know or know of?**

• **How has God taken care of you?**

Say: **No matter how hard something may seem to us, God can do it. We can trust him to take care of us all the time because he will never let us down.**

Bless You

(Jesus Blesses Children)

Mark 10:13-16

Energy Level

High Energy

This game will help children understand Jesus loves them and wants to bless them.

Supply List

☐ soft foam or rubber ball, one per every ten kids

The Game

Divide your group into teams of ten or fewer children each. Each team will play the game separately and will need a fairly large open space to play. Within each team, have children number off one through ten (or whatever number is appropriate). Each team will designate one person as "It." One way to choose "It" is to have the person with the next birthday fill the role.

"It" will toss the ball into the air and call out a number. The person whose number is called must try to catch the ball while all the other children scatter. When the children whose number was called have the ball in their hands, they must shout "Bless you!" The other children will stop scattering and freeze where they are standing. The child with the ball then throws or rolls the ball in an attempt to tag another child below the waist. If he or she succeeds, the child who was tagged becomes "It" and is the new thrower. If the child misses, he or she must retrieve the ball and become the new thrower for the next round. Play until everyone has had a turn to be "It."

Post-Game Discussion Questions

After playing this game, ask your students to sit down in groups of three and discuss:

• **How does it make you feel when you are chosen in a game? Why?**

• **What do you think it means to be "blessed"?**

• **Finish this phrase: "I am special to Jesus because…"**

Say: **The disciples wanted the children to "scatter" and leave Jesus alone. They thought the adults were more important. But Jesus loved the children, and he wanted to bless them because they were special to him. Jesus wants to bless his children today, too.**

Temple Bowling

(Jesus Clears the Temple)

John 2:13-22

Energy Level

Medium Energy

This game will help children discover God wants his house to be a place of worship.

Supply List

❏ paper egg cartons, two for each bowling pin you make

❏ masking tape

❏ black marker

❏ soft ball

The Game

Stand two closed egg cartons on end with the bottoms against each other. Wrap one or two strips of masking tape around both cartons to hold them together securely. Make four or five "bowling pins" this way, and write one of the following words on each: "doves," "sheep," "cattle," or "money-changers." (Paper towel rolls also work, but they tip over more easily.)

To play, set the cartons up on end and let the children take turns rolling the ball at them to see how many they can knock down. As the children bowl, remind them that the words on the pins are some of the things Jesus cleared out of the Temple. Play until every child has had two or three turns rolling the ball. If you have a large group of children, you may want to make more than one set of bowling pins so the children can play in small groups.

Post-Game Discussion Questions

After playing this game, ask your students to sit down in groups of three and discuss:

• How did you "clear out" the bowling pins? How is that like what Jesus did to the money-changers in the Temple?

• How would you feel if strangers came into your house and set up a flea market? Explain.

• How do you think you should treat God's house, our church?

• What are some things you can do to keep God's house a place of worship?

Say: Jesus was angry when he saw that some people were using God's house, the Temple, to buy and sell things. Jesus wanted God's house to be a place of worship, so he chased the merchants out of the Temple. We need to treat God's house—our church—as a place of worship too.

Money Hunt

(A Widow's Giving)

Mark 12:41-44
Energy Level
Medium Energy

This game will help your kids discover how to give to God as they explore the story of the widow's offering.

Supply List
❑ fake hundred-dollar bills, five of the same color for each group of up to five students—use a different color for each group (If bills don't come in colors, create your own and copy it on different colors of paper.)

❑ gold star stickers, one per group of up to five students

❑ tape (optional)

The Game

Before the game, place a gold star sticker on one of the bills of each different color. Then hide and/or tape all the bills in "hiding" places around your meeting area, but where it's possible for students to find them. Place the bills with the gold stars farthest away from the starting point of the hunt.

Divide your students into groups of up to five children each. Assign each group one of the colors used for the bills. Explain to groups that they are to search for hundred-dollar bills of that color and collect all that they find. Also explain that the bill with the gold star is the most important one of all. When they find it, they must return to you immediately and celebrate their great fortune!

Give groups five minutes to search (or more or less, depending on the size of your group and meeting area). When all the groups have returned, celebrate together. If a group was not able to find its gold-star bill, have the others help them find it so that all of the gold-star bills are returned.

Post-Game Discussion Questions

After playing this game, ask students to sit in their groups and discuss:

• How did you feel when you found the bill with the gold star? Why?

• In the Bible story, why was the widow's offering worth more than the rich people's offerings?

• Why did the widow give everything she had?

Say: **God wants us to give from our hearts. That we give is good, but what matters more is that we give because we love God.**

Concentration Conversation

(Jesus Teaches Us to Pray)

> ## Matthew 6:5-13
> ## Energy Level
> Low Energy
> Children will play a zany acting game and learn that Jesus taught us how to pray.
>
> ## Supply List
> ☐ two chairs

The Game

Set two chairs close together, facing each other.

Say: **Let's play a wacky acting game. Two of you will act out a scene I give you. But here's the twist: The** *rest* **of you will tell the actors what to say next. We'll take turns.**

Separate your audience into two groups, and assign one group to each actor. Announce the situation, assign a group to each part, and determine which actor will start. Then have children in the audience take turns instructing the actors what to say. The actors will repeat what's called out. Remind your audience that they can provide funny lines, but all suggestions must be kind and God-honoring.

Choose a scene from the scene starters below, or make up one of your own. Continue for a minute or so, then change actors and either continue the scene or switch to a new one. Repeat until everyone has had a turn to act.

Scene Starters:
• A child approaches a grouchy cashier to buy a candy bar.
• Two children have to decide who gets the first turn at a video game.
• A parent tells a child to turn off the TV and clean his or her bedroom.
• A teacher catches a student cheating on a test.
• Two children are riding bikes and one child gets a flat tire.

Post-Game Discussion Questions

After this dramatic masterpiece, discuss:

• **What was it like to have to be taught what to say? Why?**

• **Have you ever been in a conversation in which you didn't know what you should say next? How did you feel?**

• **Do you ever wonder about what to say to God when you pray?**

Say: **Jesus' friends weren't sure what they should say to God when they were praying, so they asked for Jesus' help. Jesus was happy to teach them how to talk with God and be friends with him. Jesus teaches us how to talk with God too.**

I Spy

(Zacchaeus Sees Jesus)

Luke 19:1-10
Energy Level
Low Energy
This lighthearted game engages students with the story of Jesus and Zacchaeus. It could be played indoors, outdoors, or while traveling.

Supply List
❏ none needed

The Game

Say: **Zacchaeus climbed up in a tree so he could get a better view of Jesus. And Jesus picked Zacchaeus out of the crowd to have dinner with him. Let's test our own vision with a game of I Spy.**

Choose a volunteer to begin as "It." Whoever is "It" needs to secretly identify an object in the room (car, area). The object must be something that everyone can see. Remind "It" not to give away the secret by looking directly at the object. "It" should begin the round by saying, "I spy something that is [name the color of the object]."

Say: **Now we get to ask questions about the secret object. Be sure to ask "yes" or "no" questions like: "Is it above our heads?" or "Is it made of plastic?"** Encourage the children to ask plenty of questions—narrowing the possibilities before they begin guessing. Once someone has accurately guessed the secret object, allow that person to take a turn being "It." Try to play the game until every child has a turn to be "It."

Post-Game Discussion Questions

After playing this game, draw the kids into a discussion using the following questions:

• **Which objects were most difficult to guess? Why?**

• **What questions were most helpful when you were guessing?**

• **Why do you think Zacchaeus wanted so badly to see Jesus?**

• **Why did Jesus go out of his way to find Zacchaeus and befriend him?**

Say: **Zacchaeus knew what was worth looking for—Jesus! And Jesus is just as precious for us to find today!**

Lost and Found

(The Parable

of the Lost Son)

Luke 15:11-32

Energy Level

Medium Energy

As they explore the story of the prodigal son, your kids will discover God loves each of us.

Supply List

☐ Bible

☐ eleven index cards

☐ pen

The Game

Write the following information on eleven index cards, one "bullet" per card:

• Luke 15:11-12. Act like the younger son: Turn to your father (the person next to you) and hold out your hands as if you're asking for money.

• Luke 15:12b. Act like the father: Act like you're handing money to your son (the next person in line). You should have a sad look on your face.

• Luke 15:13. Act like the younger son: Pretend to party and act like you're throwing money around and handing it to all of the people in line.

• Luke 15:14. Act like the younger son: Look sad and turn your pockets inside out to show you don't have anything. Turn to someone near you and hold out your hands, begging for money.

• Luke 15:15-16. Act like the younger son: Get down on your hands and knees and pretend to eat pig food.

• Luke 15:17-20a. Act like the younger son, traveling back home to your father. Shield your eyes with your hand as you walk in place, looking toward home.

• Luke 15:20. Act like the father: Hug your son (the next person in line) and look very happy.

• Luke 15:21. Act like the younger son: Kneel in front of your father (the next person in line) and look sad.

• Luke 15:22-24. Act like the father: Put shoes on the feet of your son (the next person in line) and a ring on his finger.

• Luke 15:25-30. Act like the older brother: Fold your arms and make an ugly face at your father (the next person in line).

• Luke 15:31-32. Act like the father and hug both of your sons (the people on either side of you).

Explain to your students that you're going to have them do a simple relay in which they act out the story of the prodigal son. Have them line up shoulder to shoulder. Explain that you'll give the first person a Bible and an index card. He or she must look up the Scripture (using the table of contents is perfectly fine!), read it aloud, pass the Bible to the next person, and then do what the card says. When this person has finished, you will give the next person the next index card. Continue in this manner until the entire story has been told.

If you get to the end of the line before the story is finished, start over again at the beginning of the line. If you have more than eleven students, have them repeat the story until everyone has had a turn to be involved.

Post-Game Discussion Questions

Ask students to take a seat and then discuss:

• **How do you think the younger son felt when his father welcomed him home? Why?**

• **How does it make you feel to know that God loves you and he'll welcome you home no matter what you do? Why?**

Say: **God loves us; we're his children. He wants us to come home to him, and he will always welcome us with open arms.**

Stay Afloat!

(Jesus Walks on Water)

Matthew 14:22-33

Energy Level

High Energy

As they explore the story of Jesus walking on water, your kids will learn about trusting Jesus.

Supply List

❑ partially inflated air mattresses—two for each group of up to eight

❑ masking tape

The Game

Help children form groups of no more than eight people each. Put down two parallel masking tape lines on the floor about fifteen feet apart. Have all groups line up single-file behind one of the lines, and have everyone take off his or her shoes. Give each group two partially inflated air mattresses.

Say: Let's pretend that the floor is water. Your job is to get all your group members to the other side safely on the "floats" you've been given. Two people from each group will be responsible for moving these floats so that you'll always have one to step on. Those two people can walk on the floor, but the rest of you can only walk on the floats! You can't let your feet touch the floor anywhere in between the taped lines.

Ask for two volunteers from each group to move the floats. Have groups try to get everyone in their group to the other side (across the other tape line). When both groups have finished, affirm the way they worked together to accomplish the goal.

Post-Game Discussion Questions

After playing this game, ask your students to sit down in their groups and discuss:

• How did the people moving the floats make it possible for you to get to the other side?

• In the Bible story, why did Peter start to sink when he was walking on the water?

• Do you think it's easy or difficult to trust Jesus? Explain your answer.

Say: We can trust Jesus with everything that goes on in our lives, no matter how big or small. We don't need to worry about anything, because Jesus will always take care of us.

Whose Life Is It Anyway?

(Encounter With Nicodemus)

John 3:1-21
Energy Level

Medium Energy

As your children play a game about Nicodemus, they'll discover that following God is a work of the heart, not just having the right kind of head knowledge.

Supply List

❑ two sets of index cards with acting assignments written on each one (see below)

❑ whistle or bell (optional)

The Game

Write each of the following acting assignments on two separate index cards, so there are two full sets of cards: beauty queens getting ready for a pageant, football team getting revved up before a game, a race-car driver and his pit crew during a race, a cheerleading squad at a football game, a rock group performing in front of its fans. Add others you think might work well for your group.

Form students into two groups. Explain that you'll pass each group an index card with an acting assignment on it, and they'll have to act out what's on the card for as long as you designate.

Give each group a different card. Then give both groups forty-five seconds to act out what's on their cards, both groups acting at the same time. When time is up, sound the whistle or bell (or flash the lights or clap your hands or call "stop"). Pass each group a new card, and give them another forty-five seconds to act out those assignments (again different cards, but acting them out at the same time).

When you've gone through all the cards, congratulate the students on their great acting jobs.

Post-Game Discussion Questions

After playing this game, ask your students to sit down in groups of three and discuss:

• Which of the acting assignments was hardest for you? Which was easiest? Explain.

• What would have made these assignments easier?

• What did Nicodemus know about Jesus when he first met him? How do you think he knew Jesus by the end of that encounter?

• Explain the difference between knowing about a person, and actually knowing the person.

• How is that like knowing *about* God versus really *knowing* God?

Say: Nicodemus knew about Jesus but he didn't really *know* him—not at first, anyway. We can read *about* Jesus, but really getting to *know* Jesus through faith is what counts most!

Bucket Brigade

(A Samaritan Woman)

John 4:5-42

Energy Level

Medium Energy

As kids work together to move water, they'll discover God wants to share his living water with everyone.

Supply List

❑ two large buckets, one half-full of water

❑ paper cups, one for each child

❑ kitchen timer

❑ plastic sheet to protect the floor (optional)

The Game

Fill one of the buckets halfway with water. Place the two buckets on the ground about ten feet apart (adjust the distance if you have lots of kids). If you are playing the game indoors, consider laying a plastic sheet on the floor. You can purchase one cheaply in the paint section of a hardware store.

Say: **The Samaritan woman wanted to let all of her friends know about Jesus' "living water."** Jesus told her that being friends with him was like enjoying a cool, refreshing glass of water. The woman wanted to share her joy with everyone she knew. Let's play a game to get us thinking about the people we can share living water with.

Have the children stand in a straight line between the two buckets. Give each child a paper cup. Say: **Let's pretend this bucket of water is Jesus' living water. The empty bucket will be our friends who don't know Jesus yet. Let's try to move as much of the water as we can in three minutes. When I say "go," the person standing closest to the water will scoop water out of the bucket and share it with the person standing next in line. Keep passing the water from person to person until it reaches the empty bucket. Let's see how much water we can move.**

Set the kitchen timer for three minutes, and shout "go." When the time is up, gather the children around the second bucket and celebrate how much water they moved.

Post-Game Discussion Questions

After playing this game, ask your students to sit down in groups of three and discuss:

• Why do you think the Samaritan woman wanted to share Jesus' friendship with all her friends?

• Why is it important for you to tell all your friends about Jesus?

• Who can you share Jesus with this week?

Say: **It's a wonderful thing to be friends with Jesus! We need to be like the Samaritan woman and tell everyone we know about Jesus' love.**

Welcome to the Neighborhood

(The Good Samaritan)

Luke 10:25-37

Energy Level

Low Energy

As you interact with the parable of the good Samaritan, your kids will learn about what it means to love other people more than themselves.

Supply List

❑ graham crackers, four to five full crackers per child

❑ frosting or cream cheese, one small bowl per group

❑ plastic knives, one per child

❑ paper plates, one per child

❑ decorative edible ornaments (cinnamon candies, pretzels, licorice, gummy items, jelly beans, M&M's candies, and so on)

Note: Be aware of food allergies before playing this game. Post information for parents outside your room noting what food items will be present.

The Game

Say: We're going to learn about God's definition of a neighbor. How many of you know your neighbors? Can you tell me a few things about one of your neighbors? Allow several children to give you some information about the people who live around them—people they consider their neighbors.

Then give each child a plate with four or five full graham crackers on it. Have small groups of children share a bowl of frosting or cream cheese. However, allow each child to have his or her own plastic knife. Place the decorating items in the middle of the tables.

Explain that kids will each make a house that they'll eat later. They'll use frosting as "mortar" to hold the crackers together, then decorate the house with their favorite snack items. Note: Make sure children are not licking their hands or knives during this process! And they should wash their hands before beginning.

When decorating time has passed, say: **Now everyone trade houses with your neighbor.**

After children have traded their houses, some perhaps more than once, each child should eat the "house" in front of him or her.

As children eat their snacks, say: **Today you shared your food with a person that may or may not live near you. Did you know that person is still your neighbor? Just as we traded our food today, and perhaps gave up a snack that we really wanted, the good Samaritan gave up some of his time and money to take care of someone he didn't even know. The good Samaritan** understood that God wants us to love everyone as our neighbor.

Post-Game Discussion Questions

After playing this game, ask your students to pair up with a person they traded houses with. Have the two of them discuss these questions:

• Based on our story and our game today, how would you define a *neighbor*?

• What is one thing you can do this week to fulfill Jesus' command to "love your neighbor as yourself"?

Spitball Float

(Jesus Raises Lazarus)

John 11:1-45

Energy Level

Medium Energy
As your kids explore the story of Jesus raising Lazarus from the dead, they'll discover just how powerful God is.

Supply List

❏ disposable cups filled full with water, one for each child
❏ straws, one for each child
❏ paper towels

The Game

Pass out a cup (full of water), a straw, and a small scrap of paper towel (approximately a 2x2-inch square) to each child. First have students wad up the scrap of paper towel into a ball. Then have students each put the straw in the cup, hold it close to his or her mouth, and hold the paper-towel ball in the other hand, ready to drop it in the cup. Explain that on the count of three, they are to take a deep breath, drop the ball in the cup, and blow into the straw to keep the ball afloat as long as they can on that one breath. When any kids run out of breath, have them cheer on the others who are still trying to keep their balls afloat.

After all students have run out of breath, say: **You did a great job keeping your paper balls afloat for as long as you could. You've got powerful lungs! But we don't have much power; we've all got to stop and take a breath sometime.**

We have a little bit of power—but Jesus has a *lot* of power!

Post-Game Discussion Questions

After playing this game, discuss the following questions with your students:

• **Did you keep the paper ball afloat as long as you thought you could? Explain.**

• **How do you think Jesus was able to raise Lazarus from the dead even though Jesus was human?**

• **Where have you seen God's power shown?**

Say: **You were only able to keep the paper ball afloat for as long as you could breathe out. As humans, we can only do so much. Jesus was human, too, but he also had the power of God...and with it he did amazing things—like bringing Lazarus back to life. God's power is really incredible!**

Conveyor Coat Covering

(Jesus Enters Jerusalem)

Matthew 21:1-11

Energy Level

High Energy

Children will act out part of Jesus' triumphal entry and experience what it means to give God worship.

Supply List

☐ old shirts, one per child (Check your church's supply closet for old shirts that have been used as art smocks. You can also ask for donations, or purchase the shirts cheaply at a thrift shop.)

For safety's sake, play this game in a carpeted room.

The Game

Say: **When Jesus entered Jerusalem on the day we celebrate as Palm Sunday, the people honored Jesus by giving him an awesome parade. Let's act out the parade with a fun game.**

Ask for a volunteer to play the role of Jesus' donkey. Give each of the other children a shirt. Say: **When I say "go," our pretend donkey will start to move around the room on all fours. If**
you are holding a shirt, it's your job to make sure that the donkey always has a shirt in front of him or her to walk on. After the donkey passes over your shirt, pick it up and get back in front of the donkey.

Donkey, if the crowd can't get shirts in front of you fast enough, and you have nowhere to go, I want you to start braying like a donkey. Let out a loud "hee-haw" to let everyone know to speed up the coat conveyor belt.

Shout "go!" and let the children play for a few minutes. Frequently switch who gets to be the donkey. After everyone has had a chance to be the donkey, gather the children in a circle around you.

Post-Game Discussion Questions

Lead a discussion using these questions:

• **Was it easy or hard to keep up with the donkey? Explain.**

• **How hard do you think it was for the crowd to give Jesus his big parade? Why?**

• **How much effort do you think we should put into worshipping Jesus? Explain.**

Say: **Jesus is God's Son. He is amazing. He loves us and wants to be our friend. We can let Jesus know how much we love him by giving him our worship. We can be happy to worship Jesus—even when it takes a lot of our energy.**

Wipe Tag

(Jesus Washes

the Disciples' Feet)

John 13:1-17

Energy Level

High Energy

Children will play a zany game in which they try to avoid letting someone else wash their feet.

Supply List

☐ box of baby wipes

The Game

Have all of the children take off their shoes and socks and set them aside. Girls wearing tights may still play, but caution them to be careful not to slip. Have the children sit in a circle on the floor. Say: **Peter didn't want Jesus to wash his feet. He thought that Jesus was too special to serve him in that way. Let's play a game in which we act like Peter.**

Help the children find partners. Instruct pairs to stand facing each other so their fingers just barely touch with their arms outstretched. Give each child a baby wipe. Explain that each person's goal is to tag his or her partner's feet with the baby wipe, without being tagged by his or her partner. To keep the game safe, tell the children that kicking is not allowed. If you are limited in space, have the children play two at a time. Play for a minute, and then have the children find new partners. Play several rounds, as long as the children's interest remains. If you have an uneven number of children, be sure that the group of three consists of different children each round.

Post-Game Discussion Questions

Gather the children around you. Collect the baby wipes so they won't be a distraction. Discuss these questions:

• **Was it easy or hard to avoid having your feet wiped? Explain.**

• **Why do you think Peter didn't want Jesus to wash his feet?**

• **Why is it important to be like Jesus and serve others?**

Say: **Jesus wanted to teach his disciples an important lesson. He was willing to serve others. Jesus was the most important person in the room that night. If he was willing to serve others, we can be happy to serve others as well.**

Blind Leading the Mob

(Jesus Is Tried and Crucified)

Luke 23:1-49
Energy Level
High Energy

This game will help your kids discover how a mob convinced Pilate to have Jesus crucified despite the fact that Pilate found Jesus innocent of the charges brought against him.

Supply List
☐ clean cloth blindfolds, one per student

The Game

Play this game in a confined area such as a small classroom. Blindfold a volunteer who'll start the game as a one-person mob.

Say: **Our blindfolded volunteer is going to try to tag you. If you're tagged I will then blindfold you and the two of you will interlock arms and try to tag** another person. Those of you who are not blindfolded must try to stay away from our volunteer, or the growing mob. However, if you're not part of the mob, you must hop on one foot in order to remain in the game. The blindfolded people don't have to hop. Are you ready? Go! Allow the kids to play until the majority of the kids have become part of the mob with interlocking arms.

Post-Game Discussion Questions

After playing this game, ask your students to sit down in groups of three and discuss:

• **How easy or difficult was it to stay away from the mob when it was one person? How about as it kept growing? Explain.**

• **How was the growing mob like a mob of people who egg on each other to do bad things?**

• **Why were the religious leaders of Jesus' day so interested in crucifying Jesus even though a government leader like Pilate believed that Jesus was innocent?**

Say: **The religious leaders wanted Jesus crucified because he claimed to be God. Of course, Jesus really *is* God, but those religious leaders didn't believe it.**

Impossible? Knot!

(Jesus Rises

From the Dead)

Matthew 28:1-10
Energy Level

Low Energy

This game will seem impossible to kids at first, just as Jesus' resurrection must have seemed impossible at the time. But kids will realize that the game is possible, just as Jesus rising from the dead was possible because Jesus is God!

Supply List

❑ three-foot length of string or rope for every two kids

The Game

Have kids form pairs, and give each pair a length of rope or string.

Challenge kids to hold one end of the rope in each hand and tie a knot without letting go of the ends. Let one partner attempt to tie the knot as the other partner cheers him or her on. Then let partners switch roles.

Play for several minutes. If anyone figures out the solution, have that pair sit down until the end of the game. Then they can explain the solution to the rest of the class. If no one comes up with the solution, explain it yourself: The knot can be tied by crossing your arms over your chest, so that one hand is in front of your arms and the other is behind or below them, almost like crossing your arms twice. Then lean over and pick up the ends of the rope with your arms still crossed. When you unfold your arms, a knot is automatically tied in the rope.

Post-Game Discussion Questions

After playing the game, have partners sit down and discuss:

• Did you think it would be possible to tie a knot with the rules I described? Why or why not?

• Do you think people thought it was possible for Jesus to rise from the dead? Why or why not?

• How do you explain Jesus rising from the dead? How is that different from being able to tie a knot in this game?

Say: Being able to tie a knot in this game was just a trick. But Jesus rising from the dead was real!

Sight Seeing

(Jesus Appears to Mary)

John 20:1-18

Energy Level

Medium Energy

As kids explore Jesus' appearance to Mary, they will learn that God always keeps his word, no matter how hard it is to believe.

Supply List

❏ grocery bag for each team of four or five kids

❏ one scavenger hunt list per team of four or five kids; the list should include the following: a pebble, a white napkin or piece of cloth, a tissue, a handful of dirt, a ruler, and a newspaper. (You will likely need to strategically plant some of these items—one per team—prior to the game.)

The Game

Say: **Today we're going to learn that seeing** *can* **be believing. It's important that we pay attention to the things God puts in our paths each day, because we never know what he has in store for us. Just like Mary, we may be very surprised by what we see!**

Help the children form groups of four or five. Give each team a grocery bag to take with them on their scavenger hunt. Give them approximately ten to fifteen minutes to find the items on the list and return to your room. Say: **You have ten minutes to gather the items on your team's list. That means you will need to be back here at** [state the time kids should be back]. **If you find more than one of an item on your list, leave the extra item where you found it.**

Shorten or lengthen the time depending on your location, availability of supplies, time constraints, and so on. You want the teams to feel pressure to finish, but not be overwhelmed.

When the children return, talk about the items they found and how they could remind students of the time when Jesus appeared to Mary. Affirm all the children's ideas. If they need help getting started, offer some of these ideas:

The pebble could remind us of the stone that was in front of Jesus' grave.

The napkin or cloth could remind us of the grave clothes that Jesus left behind.

The tissue could remind us that Mary cried when she couldn't find Jesus.

The dirt could remind us that Mary mistook Jesus for the gardener.

The ruler could remind us that Mary called Jesus "Teacher."

The newspaper could remind us that Mary shared the exciting news with the disciples.

Post-Game Discussion Questions

After playing this scavenger hunt game, ask your students to sit down together and discuss:

• **Do you think Mary knew that she was talking to angels at Jesus' grave? Explain your answer.**

• **Why do you think Mary mistook Jesus for the gardener?**

• **Describe a time when you saw something that was hard to believe. What made you believe it was true?**

Say: **This account of Jesus' appearance to Mary reminds us that God will always keep his word, no matter how hard it is to believe.**

Case of the Missing Person

(Jesus Returns to Heaven)

Acts 1:1-11

Energy Level

Low Energy

In this game, kids will try to figure out who's missing from the class. They'll get an idea of how some people must have felt after Jesus returned to heaven.

Supply List

☐ none needed

The Game

Clear the center of your room of obstacles. Have everyone stand in the center of the room and close his or her eyes. Tell kids to keep their eyes closed until you say it's OK to open them. Gently take each person by the shoulders and lead each one to a new location in the room, making sure each child faces in a different direction than he or she did at first.

Choose one child to hide in the room or just outside the door. Whisper to that child to open his or her eyes as you lead the child either out of the room or to a closet or other hiding place where others can't see him or her.

When one child is hidden, tell kids they can open their eyes. See if they can figure out who's missing. (If you have a small group where the answer will be obvious, change the game so that an item in the room is missing.) Play several rounds of the game if time permits, hiding a new child each time.

Post-Game Discussion Questions

After playing the game, ask your students to sit down in groups of three and discuss:

• **Were you surprised at how hard it was to detect who was missing? Explain.**

• **What do you think Jesus' followers thought when he returned to heaven? How do you think they felt?**

• **Why do you think Jesus came to earth in the first place? Why do you think he returned to heaven?**

Say: **Jesus came to earth to offer us the gift of salvation and forgiveness. He'll return one day to gather his believers, who will live forever with him in heaven!**

Listen Up!

(Jesus Sends Power From God)

John 16:13-15; Acts 2:1-21

Energy Level

Low Energy

This game will help kids remember to listen for the Holy Spirit.

Supply List

❑ wire clothes hanger for every two kids

❑ five-foot length of string for every two kids

❑ chair or table

The Game

Help kids form pairs. Give each pair a wire clothes hanger and a length of string. Demonstrate how to tie the middle of the string to the hook of the hanger. Show kids how to wrap one end of the string several times around one index finger, and the other end of the string around the other index finger. Show the kids how to place the ends of their index fingers lightly in their ears and bend over carefully. Then let the hanger hit lightly against a chair or table. Surprisingly, the sound you will hear will be that of church bells or an old-fashioned clock.

Ask kids what they think they'll hear when they perform the experiment themselves. Then let partners take turns doing the trick. After everyone has had a turn, collect the supplies.

Post-Game Discussion Questions

After playing the game, ask your students to sit down in groups of four and discuss:

• Did you hear what you expected to hear? Explain.

• Does God always communicate with you in the ways that you expect? Explain.

• How can you be more open to hearing and obeying the Holy Spirit?

Say: **Sometimes God speaks to us in unexpected ways. God sends the Holy Spirit to remind us of what Jesus said, to comfort us, and to help us. We can all be more open to hearing what the Holy Spirit has to say.**

On the Defense

(Apostles Defend Their Faith)

Acts 5:12-42

Energy Level

High Energy

This game will help your kids discover how God helps us stand up for what we believe as they explore how the apostles defended their faith.

Supply List

☐ lots of newspaper

☐ masking tape

The Game

Place a line of masking tape on the floor across the middle of the play area, dividing the room into two equal spaces. Then put two more parallel lines of masking tape on the floor perpendicular to the center line, about three feet from each edge of the play area. These side areas will be "out-of-bounds."

Divide the children into two teams of equal size, and have each team take one side of the play area. Explain the boundaries and the out-of-bounds areas. Pass out a pile of newspapers to each group. Designate one group as the "Apostles" and the other group the "Sadducees."

Say: **We know from the Bible that the apostles had to stand up to the**

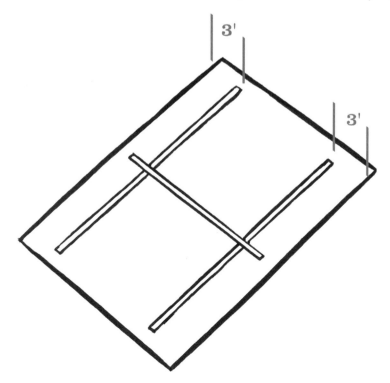

Sadducees and defend their faith. In this game, it's the Sadducees' job to throw paper wads at the Apostles, and it's the Apostles' job to hit away the paper wads into the out-of-bounds areas. Any paper wads that fall on the Sadducees' side of the play area but not in the out-of-bounds sections can be picked up and thrown again, but paper wads hit into the out-of-bounds sections cannot be reused. The Apostles can use their newspaper however they want in order to hit away the paper wads (they can make bats, shields, or "golf clubs" out of the newspapers). But they can't use their hands, only the newspapers.

Let students play for about five minutes, then have groups switch roles so that the Apostles get a chance to be the Sadducees and vice versa. Let them play for another five minutes. When time is up, ask the children to help you clean up the newspaper.

Post-Game Discussion Questions

After playing this game, ask your students to sit down in their groups and discuss:

• How did you feel as an Apostle having to fight off the paper wads? Explain.

• How is that like having to defend your faith?

• How can knowing the Bible help us defend our faith?

Say: **Just as God gave the apostles strength to stand up against their critics, God also gives us strength to stand up against people who criticize us for believing in God. We have to keep reading our Bibles and understand God's promises so that we'll remember them when we have to defend our faith too.**

Captives, Guards, and Angels

(An Angel Frees Peter From Jail)

Acts 12:1-18

Energy Level

High Energy
This game will help kids understand the power of God as they enjoy team play and explore the story of Peter being freed from jail.

Supply List

❑ masking tape

The Game

Before playing, establish boundaries for the game. You'll need a large space with three areas marked out in concentric circles. The inner circle is the prison, the second circle is the guard zone, and the outer circle is the angel zone. Mark the boundaries of each circle with masking tape on the floor.

Gather your students, and say: **For this game, we need three teams of equal size—Captives, Guards, and Angels.** Help the students divide, and send them to their zones.

The object of the game is for the Angels to free all the Captives from the prison. Point out the three zones. Explain that the Angels can free Captives if they safely make it through the guard zone and tag a Captive in the prison. After tagging a Captive, they

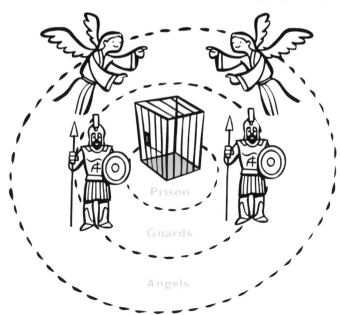

Prison

Guards

Angels

both have safe passage back to the angel zone. The freed Captive is now an Angel and should begin working to free more Captives. If a Guard tags an Angel in the guard zone, that Angel becomes a Captive and must be freed by another Angel. Guards may not tag Angels in the angel zone or the prison.

Try to play the game three times—allowing the kids to experience the different roles.

Post-Game Discussion Questions

After playing this game, ask your students to sit down in groups of three and discuss:

• **How do you think Peter might have felt in prison? Why?**

• **What did it feel like to be an Angel and free a Captive in this game? Explain.**

• **How did Peter respond when the angel freed him from prison?**

Say: **God uses his power in creative ways to bring us out of danger and keep us safe.**

Purple People

(Lydia's Conversion)

Acts 16:9-15

Energy Level

Medium Energy

As they play this game, your students will explore the story of Lydia's conversion—and discover how God can transform their lives.

Supply List

☐ lots of purple paper
☐ several rolls of tape
☐ instant-print camera with film (optional)

The Game

Help students form groups of five or six, and give each group lots of purple paper and tape. Say: **Your job is to choose one member of your group to be completely covered in purple. You can be as creative as you want to be, but try to cover as much of the person as you can in purple paper, as long as the person can still breathe!**

Explain that this is not a race, but they do have only five minutes to work. When time is up, have each group model its purple person. Take pictures if you want, and be sure to show the pictures to the purple people so they can see what they looked like.

Post-Game Discussion Questions

After playing this game, have the children remove the paper from the purple people. Then ask them to sit down in their groups and discuss:

• **How were the volunteers changed in this game?**

• **How was Lydia changed in the Bible story?**

• **What does it mean to change and become a follower of God?**

• **Has God changed you? Tell about that experience.**

Say: **God changed Lydia's life when Paul shared the story of God's love with her. God is so powerful that he can change anyone. We only need to be open to God's changes. Let's always be open to God because he will always do what's best for us.**

Jail Tag

(Paul and Silas Go to Jail)

Acts 16:16-34

Energy Level

High Energy

This game will help your kids discover how it might have felt to be in prison and then freed, just like Paul and Silas.

Supply List

☐ none needed

The Game

Choose one volunteer to be the jailer and two others to be "earthquakes." Everyone else will be Paul and Silas. If you have a large group, choose one jailer per ten children.

Designate the playing area with two opposite (diagonal) corners being the "jails" and the other two corners being the "bases." The jailer should stand in the middle of the playing field. The "earthquakes" should stand one in each of the jails. All the Paul and Silas children should start out in one of the "bases."

When you say "go!" have all the Paul and Silas children attempt to run from one base to the other without being caught by the jailer. If they are tagged, they should go to one of the jails. When they get to jail, the "earthquake" will give them a gentle shake to free them. Then they can rejoin the group and continue to play.

After a few rounds, change jailers and "earthquakes" so that everyone gets a turn to play each of the different roles.

Post-Game Discussion Questions

After playing this game, ask your students to sit down in groups of three and discuss:

• Why do you think God freed Paul and Silas from jail?

• How would you have felt if you had been the jailer and you thought that all your prisoners had escaped? Explain.

• Why do you think Paul and Silas didn't run away when they had the chance?

Say: God took care of Paul and Silas, even when they were in jail. God takes care of us, too.

Shipwreck Unrace

(Paul Is Shipwrecked)

Acts 27:1-44
Energy Level

High Energy

Through this game, students will practice looking out for others, encouraging others, and reaching a common goal.

Supply List

❑ misting fan bottle (optional)

The Game

Designate one area in the room to be the "shipwreck" and another area to be the "island." Have all the kids gather around the shipwreck.

Explain that the goal is for students to "swim" to the island, but they can only arrive safely if they all touch the island at the same time. The trick of the game is to keep an eye on everyone else and encourage them along.

Assign each player a different swimming style to do as they "swim" from the shipwreck to the island.

Swimming styles you might assign include backstroke, breast stroke, sidestroke, dog paddle, tiptoeing (to keep head above water), crab-walking (along the bottom), sliding feet through the mud, whirlpool swimming (spinning), bouncing up and down on waves, riptide (two steps forward and one step back), and so on. When everyone knows his or her "stroke," show the swimmers the path they must swim, which might include a couple of trips around the classroom furniture before reaching the island. Then give the signal to begin.

As an option, you may simulate a storm at sea by using a misting fan bottle to spray water and wind on the swimmers as they travel.

When the fastest swimmers approach the island, you might need to remind them to think of ways to help or encourage the slower swimmers as they "tread water" and wait. If anyone touches the island early, tell the person that a wave has washed him or her back to sea, and then he or she has to look for a slower swimmer to swim next to. This person may keep using the same stroke but just slow it down to match the slower swimmer's pace. When all the swimmers are gathered around the island, signal them to touch it all together and give a cheer for arriving safely.

Post-Game Discussion Questions

After playing this game, ask your students to sit in groups of three and discuss:

• What made this game easier or harder as you were "swimming"?

• How do you think the people on the ship felt about Paul's continued encouragement? Why?

• What difference does it make to have others to help you or encourage you when you're doing something hard or scary?

• How can you be an encourager to people around you?

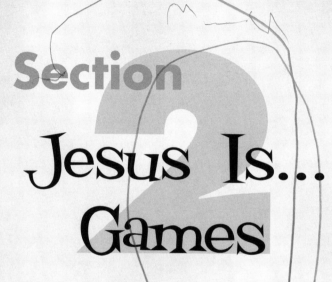

Section

2

Jesus Is...
Games

*Here are ten games to help
you connect your kids with Jesus!*

Only Jesus

(Jesus Is God's Son)

Matthew 3:16-17

Energy Level

Low Energy

Children will review what they know about Jesus and realize that only God's Son could do the things Jesus did.

Supply List

☐ Bible

The Game

Have children sit in a circle. Say: **Let's play a game in which we take turns sharing things we know about Jesus.**

Have one child start the game by turning to the person on his or her left and sharing one thing that only Jesus could do. For example, the child might say, "Jesus can walk on water." The child on the speaker's left will add, "Only God's Son can do that." That child will now turn to the person on his or her left and repeat that fact about Jesus and then add one more.

"Jesus can walk on water *and* Jesus can forgive sins." Each new speaker needs to repeat everything that has been said about Jesus and then add one more thing.

If a child is unable to remember one of the statements about Jesus, encourage the child to turn to another child for help. If a child can't think of something special about Jesus to add, encourage that child to ask another child for help as well. Keep going until every child has added a new fact about Jesus.

Post-Game Discussion Questions

After playing this game say: **Wow. You all sure remember a lot of special things about Jesus. Jesus could do things that no one else could do.**

Discuss these questions with your students:

• **Why was Jesus able to do so many special things?**

• **What's your favorite thing that Jesus ever did? Why?**

Read aloud Matthew 3:16-17. Say: **One day God told everyone that Jesus is his Son. Only God's Son could do all the special things that Jesus did.**

Safe in the Sheep Pen

(Jesus Is Seeking the Lost)

Matthew 9:35-36

Energy Level

Medium Energy

This game will help children discover Jesus seeks us because he loves us.

Supply List

☐ several chairs
☐ clean cloth blindfold

The Game

Place several chairs in a circle with the backs facing in. This will be the sheep's pen. Leave a space where the kids can move into and out of the pen.

One child will be blindfolded and designated as the Seeker. The rest of the children will scatter and walk—not run—around the Seeker saying "baa." When the seeker reaches out and touches a sheep, that sheep will go to the safety of the sheep's pen, inside the circle of chairs.

Say: **Good, you've found a sheep. Now that sheep can rest safely in the sheep's pen!** The other sheep will then have to stop and applaud, frozen in place for three seconds. The Seeker will continue until he's landed all the sheep safely in the pen. Then the game begins again with a new Seeker being blindfolded. Play until everyone has a turn to be the Seeker.

Post-Game Discussion Questions

After playing this game, ask your students to sit down in groups of three and discuss:

• **How do you think a shepherd cares for his sheep?**

• **Where do you keep things you care about?**

• **How does Jesus show that he loves us?**

Say: **Jesus seeks us to be his children because he loves us. He wants us to be safe.**

Grape Game

(Jesus Is Compassionate)

Mark 1:40-45

Energy Level

Medium Energy

As your kids play this game, they'll see how Jesus showed compassion when he cured a man of leprosy.

Supply List

☐ two clean buckets
☐ two large mixing bowls
☐ two bunches of grapes, washed and plucked loose
☐ enough ice to fill the buckets
☐ two pairs of child's gloves (not knit gloves—ice might stick to them)
☐ newspapers or trash bags to protect floor

The Game

Before students arrive, mix loose grapes and ice in the buckets. Place newspapers or trash bags under the buckets to protect the floor. Place a pair of child's gloves and a large mixing bowl next to each bucket.

Divide children into two groups. Ask each group to line up single file about ten feet away from the buckets.

Say: **Let's pretend we're stranded on a desert island and the only thing we have to eat are grapes. We don't** want any of our friends to go hungry, so it's your group's job to find as many grapes as you can in your bucket and give them to the other group.

Explain that when a group finds a grape, kids are to place the grapes in the other group's mixing bowl. Ask group members to take turns looking for grapes, to find up to five, then to run and place the grapes in the other group's bowl. Make sure everyone gets a turn. Do this until most (or all) of the grapes have been found.

When they've finished, wash the grapes, and let children enjoy the snack provided by the other group.

Post-Game Discussion Questions

After playing this game, discuss the following questions with your students:

• **In our game, how were you kind to the other group?**

• **In the Bible story, how was Jesus kind to the man with leprosy?**

• **When is it easy to be kind to others? When is it hard to be kind?**

• **Why does Jesus want us to be kind to others?**

Say: **Jesus showed kindness to the man with leprosy by healing him. There's another word for what Jesus had: *compassion*. Jesus showed *compassion* all throughout his time on earth, and he teaches us how to show God's love to others by showing compassion for them. Let's think of one thing we can do this week to be kind and show compassion to someone else.**

Life-Size Kindness

(Jesus Is Kind)

Luke 6:35
Energy Level
Low Energy
This game will help the children discover Jesus was kind and instructed us to be kind to others.

Supply List
❏ twenty-five sheets of construction paper
❏ dice
❏ marker
❏ masking tape

The Game

Lay the construction paper on the floor in a large circle, using a small piece of masking tape to hold each sheet in place. Your children will become playing pieces in a life-size board game, stepping from one sheet of paper to another.

Use the marker to write an "S" on one sheet. This will be where kids start. A child will stand there, roll one die, and then before advancing the number of spaces indicated on the die, will first tell how he or she could show kindness in a situation you describe. There are no wrong or right answers; encourage kids to think of creative, realistic ways they could show kindness in each situation.

After a child gives an answer, have the child advance the indicated number of spaces. Spaces are in a circle shape so there's no "finish" line. Play until everyone has had several turns or has been around the circle at least once.

Here are several suggestions for situations you might use; add your own as well:

• **You see an elderly lady drop her bag of groceries.**

• **A new boy arrives at school, and he cannot speak English very well.**

• **Mom is busy making supper when your little sister begins to fuss.**

• **Your friend has lost her kitten.**

• **You see paper on the floor at church.**

• **The elderly man next door is sick.**

• **Your little brother is having a hard time with his math problems.**

• **A family in your neighborhood has lost their house in a fire.**

• **The floor needs to be vacuumed.**

• **A new girl attends your Sunday school class for the first time.**

Post-Game Discussion Questions

After playing this game, ask your students to sit down in groups of three and discuss:

• Describe a time when someone was kind to you. How did you feel?

• Describe a way that Jesus is kind to you. How do you feel?

• What are some ways you can show kindness at school?

Say: **When we show kindness to others, we are following the example that Jesus set for us. The Bible tells us that Jesus is kind even to people who don't like him.**

Race to Draw Power and Thanks

(Jesus Is Powerful)

Luke 17:11-19
Energy Level

Low Energy

Through a drawing race, kids will discover Jesus' power to heal ten lepers and will think of things for which they can thank Jesus.

Supply List

❑ two easels (or a chalkboard or white board)

❑ poster board or newsprint

❑ markers

The Game

Form kids into two groups, and have each group sit by an easel with poster board or newsprint. Place easels at opposite ends of your game area.

Say: **Jesus showed his power when he healed ten men with leprosy. Then one of the men showed his gratitude when he came back to thank Jesus. In this game, you'll each get to draw two pictures—one that shows Jesus' power and one that shows something you're thankful for.**

Take a moment for kids to brainstorm what they might draw. For Jesus' power, kids might draw anything in creation that impresses them, such as the power of a volcano or the intricacy of a butterfly. Or they might choose to draw something that represents an answer to prayer—for example, a school building if they'd asked Jesus to help with a problem at school. Children could draw anything that amazes them about Jesus and what he's done.

For pictures representing thanks, the kids could draw anything they're thankful for—family, food, money, a fun place they got to visit, and so on.

Say: **Let's see how fast we can think of, draw, and guess your ideas!**

Assign one easel for the "power" pictures and the other easel for the "thanks" pictures. Have both groups begin at the same time, with one child from each group drawing while others in the group call out guesses of what the picture is. The kids at the "thanks" easel will draw pictures of what they're thankful for, while the kids at the "power" easel draw pictures illustrating Jesus' power. As soon as a sketch is guessed, the child who drew it will move to join the other group while the next child sketches. Gradually switch all the players, though not at the same time. Play until kids have drawn at both easels and moved back to their original sides.

Post-Game Discussion Questions

After playing this game, ask your students to sit in small groups and discuss:

• What were some new or different things you learned about Jesus' power from this game? Can you think of more that were too hard to draw?

• Why is it important to take time to thank Jesus?

• What can we do to keep ourselves looking for Jesus' power and remind ourselves to thank him?

Say: **Isn't it great that Jesus can do so much and gives us so much? This week, keep looking for things to praise and thank him for.**

Lifelines
(Jesus Is Our Savior)

John 3:16-17
Energy Level
Medium Energy
This game will help kids see Jesus is our rescuer and offers us a lifeline when we're trapped in sin.

Supply List
❏ jump-ropes, one for every four kids

The Game

Have kids form groups of four, and give one person in each group a jump-rope. Those kids will be the Rescuers. Say: **Often when a person is trapped somewhere and can't get out, rescuers throw the person a lifeline to hold onto while they're being pulled to safety. In this game, the jump-ropes will be the lifelines.**

Have Rescuers stand on one side of the room and other kids mingle around at the other end of the room until kids are no longer in their groups. Ask everyone except the Rescuers to kneel and close their eyes. Explain that at your signal, those without lifelines (that's everyone but the rescuers!) will silently raise their hands. Rescuers will speed walk to their group members and rescue them one by one.

To rescue a group member, the Rescuer will tap the person on the shoulder, and help the person stand up and hold the lifeline. Then the Rescuer will usher the rescued person across the room to the safety zone. Kids can open their eyes only when they've reached the safety zone.

If you have time, play several rounds, having kids change groups and roles. This game is best played in a large room or outdoors. If you're playing in a classroom, make sure all obstacles have been removed from the center of the room.

Post-Game Discussion Questions

After playing the game, ask your students to sit down in their original groups and discuss:

• What was it like waiting to be rescued?

• How did you feel when you were rescued?

• How is being saved by Jesus like being thrown a lifeline?

Say: **Just as people who are trapped need a lifeline, we're all trapped in sin. Jesus is our rescuer, our Savior who throws us the lifeline of salvation.**

Five in a Row

(Jesus Is Forgiving)

John 8:3-11

Energy Level

Low Energy

This game will help children to discover that when Jesus forgives them, their sins are forgotten.

Supply List

☐ none needed

The Game

Choose five children to stand before the class. Then have them leave the room, mix up, and return in a different order. Let the other children try to remember what order they were in before they left the room. When they figure out the correct order, choose five other children to repeat the game. Emphasize that we have to think hard in order to remember.

Post-Game Discussion Questions

After playing this game, ask your students to sit down in their groups of five and discuss:

• **How did you remember what order your friends were in when we played our game?**

• **What are things you wish other people would remember about you? What are things you wish they** *wouldn't* **remember?**

• **What happens when you forgive somebody?**

• **What happens when Jesus forgives us?**

Say: **Sometimes when people remember us, they remember all the** *wrong* **things—only the things we wish they'd forget. But Jesus, when he forgives us, doesn't remember what we've done. He throws all our sins away!**

Do You Measure Up?

(Jesus Is Love)

John 15:9-13
Energy Level

Low Energy

This game will help children realize that Jesus' love for them is too great to be measured.

Supply List

- ❏ measuring tape
- ❏ paper and pencil
- ❏ masking tape

The Game

Put a line of masking tape on the floor. Ask children to stand in a parallel line behind it. Then say: **When it's your turn, jump forward with both feet.** One at a time the children will jump forward as far as they can. If you have any helpers, have them assist you in measuring how far each child jumps, and write down the distance. Don't tell each child how far he or she jumped—it's not a competition.

When children have all had a turn to jump, add up the distances. Then say: **Wow, you jumped a total of thirteen feet, six inches** (or whatever the total is). Go on to another challenge such as jumping on one foot, jumping backward, and so on. You could also measure other distances, such as how high the children can reach or how long the line is when the children hold hands and stretch out as far as they can. Each time announce *only* the total distance that the group attained.

Post-Game Discussion Questions

After playing this game, ask your students to sit down in groups of three and discuss:

• **How did we measure how far you jumped?**

• **What are some other things that people measure?**

• **How far away are the stars?**

• **How big is Jesus' love for us?**

Say: **We can measure certain things like how far we jumped or how high we can reach, but we *cannot* measure Jesus' love for us because it's too big! Jesus loves us so much, he gave his life for us!**

Serving Up Acceptance

(Jesus Is Accepting)

Romans 15:7

Energy Level

Medium Energy

Students will display acceptance of each other through an active praise game.

Supply List

❑ inflated balloons, one for every two or three students

❑ Bible

The Game

Ask children to call out things they could compliment each other about. Suggest they think about character traits, such as friendly, happy, persistent, and so on. "Cool shoes" doesn't count!

When kids have the idea, help them form groups of two or three. Give each group an inflated balloon. Tell them to keep the balloon aloft, like a volleyball. As he or she hits the balloon to serve it back to another child, the child hitting the balloon must call out a word of praise or compliment to the child who hit the balloon last. Change who's in each group a few times to allow students to compliment as many other children as possible.

Post-Game Discussion Questions

After playing this game, ask your students to sit down in groups of three and discuss:

• **How did it feel to hear others say such nice things about you?**

• **Why is it important to tell others good things about them?**

• **How do you show that you accept someone for who he or she is?**

Read aloud Romans 15:7. Then ask:

• **According to this verse, why should we accept others?**

• **How does it make you feel to know that Jesus accepts you?**

Wordly Wise

(Jesus Is Alive)

Colossians 3:1-2

Energy Level

Low Energy

As your children are challenged to think in "heavenly" ways instead of "earthly" ways, they'll discover Jesus is alive and relates to them.

Supply List

❑ a foam ball or beanbag

The Game

Ask children to sit down in a circle around you. Say: **In a moment, I'll toss this ball to one of you. After you catch it, I'll say a word, and I want you to say back the first word that comes to your mind. Then toss the ball back to me, and I'll toss it to another person.**

Toss the ball to various children in the circle, until everyone has had a turn. You might use words like *food, sports, garden, clouds, summer, tree,* and so on. The kids will likely respond with words like *pizza, soccer, flowers, sky, vacation, leaves,* and so on.

After everyone has had a turn, say:

The Bible tells us Jesus is alive and living in heaven. Though Jesus died on the cross, he didn't stay dead. Jesus was resurrected—he came back to life!

Because Jesus is alive in heaven, let's try to think about things in heaven. Let's play our word game again, but this time I want you to think about "heavenly" words. Before you begin to toss the ball again, give some examples of how children's responses might change. For example, when you say *garden,* a student might answer *Eden* or *perfect.*

Using the same words as before, play the game again, encouraging each student to think of "heavenly" words, because Jesus is alive in heaven.

Post-Game Discussion Questions

After playing this game, ask your students to sit down in groups of three and discuss:

• **Which was easier, thinking of earthly words or heavenly words? Why do you think that's true?**

• **How do we know that Jesus is alive?**

Say: **The Bible tells us that Jesus rose again from the dead, that Jesus is alive! Lots of Jesus' friends saw him alive, and some even saw Jesus return to heaven. Let's be glad Jesus is alive!**

The Bible Is...
Games

*Help kids discover ten truths
about the Bible with these games!*

Lights... Camera... Action!

(The Bible Is Action-Packed)

Psalm 77:11-12

Energy Level

Medium Energy
This game will help your kids understand that the Bible is full of action and intrigue.

Supply List
- ❏ slips of paper
- ❏ pens or pencils
- ❏ hats or boxes
- ❏ Bibles

The Game

Begin by asking students to list action-packed Bible stories they already know. For example, David and Goliath, Noah's ark, and the parting of the Red Sea.

Ask students to form two teams.

Explain you'll play a game of "Bible Action Charades." Each team will need at least five action stories found in the Bible. Tell students they can use some of the stories mentioned, but encourage them to think of different ones. Provide Bibles for reference. Ask each team to write a description of their stories on slips of paper, and put each set of paper slips in a hat or box.

Review the rules of charades: One person from a team acts out a story without speaking, and the rest of the team gets to guess what it is. Select a team to go first, and let that team select a member to go first. Ask teams to alternate presenting stories.

Post-Game Discussion Questions

After playing this game, discuss the following questions with your students:

• **How do you feel about reading the Bible? Explain.**

• **Does it surprise you to realize that the Bible is full of so many action-packed, exciting stories? Why or why not?**

Say: **The Bible is an exciting book to read. God's story is full of action and drama. Read it today!**

Are You Up to the Challenge?

(The Bible Is Challenging—It Calls Us to Change)

Psalm 119:9-16
Energy Level
Medium Energy
This game will help your kids understand that God's Word challenges each of us to become who God wants us to be.

Supply List
❑ piece of rope or twine

The Game

Before your class meets, plan a good obstacle course. Students will travel the course while tied together, so keep that in mind.

Begin by having students stand shoulder to shoulder in a circle. Cut a piece of twine or rope that's long enough to stretch around their backs. Then have kids take two steps in toward the center of the circle. When they're as close together as they can be, wrap the rope or twine around their backs and tie it. Explain you'll lead the way as they move through an obstacle course. They'll stay tied together the whole time. Remind kids to be careful so that no one trips.

When students have completed the course, untie the group. Then discuss the following questions.

Post-Game Discussion Questions

After playing this game, ask students to discuss:

• **What was it like to do this obstacle course while you were all tied together?**

• **How did you have to change your usual behavior to complete this challenge?**

• **How might this challenge be like the challenges God gives us in the Bible?**

Say: **Just as we were challenged during this obstacle course, God challenges us in the Bible. He challenges us to become more like him as we cooperate with his purposes in our lives.**

And just as we worked together to solve our challenge today, God gives us support and guidance in his Word to help us.

Follow the Lamp

(The Bible Is God's Word)

Psalm 119:105

Energy Level

Medium Energy

Children will play a variation of Follow the Leader in a darkened room and discover how God's Word is like a lamp.

Supply List

☐ Bible

☐ flashlight

☐ optional: a black garbage bag for each window in your classroom, duct tape

The Game

Before beginning the game, clear the room of any obstacles children could stumble over in the dark. Move tables and chairs against the wall. If you can't make your classroom dark, consider taping black garbage bags over the windows.

Read Psalm 119:105 aloud. Then say: **Hmm. God's Word is like a lamp.**

That's a strange thing to say about the Bible. Let's play a game that will help us understand this verse.

Lead the children in a short game of Follow the Leader. Instruct the children to line up behind you, follow you around the room, and do whatever you do. For safety, keep your pace at a walk.

Say: **That was easy enough. Now let's make it interesting. I'm going to choose a new leader and then darken the lights. You still need to follow the leader, even though it's dark.** Choose a leader, darken the lights, and let the children play the game in the dark. Stand near the light switch and be quick to turn on the lights before the children crash into each other. Ask:

• **Is this a good way to play the game? Why or why not?**

• **What if I gave the leader some help? What if the leader had a flashlight so you had something to see?**

Turn on the flashlight, and hand it to the leader. Turn off the classroom lights.

Say: **Let's try again. The leader will walk. Stay in a line behind the leader and go wherever the leader goes.** Allow the children to play for a few minutes. Turn on the lights, stop the game, and assign a new leader. Repeat until everyone has had a turn to be the leader.

Post-Game Discussion Questions

After playing this game, ask your students to sit down in groups of three and discuss:

• **How did the flashlight make the game more fun?**

• **How is obeying God's Word like** following a flashlight in a dark room?

• **How is the Bible different from every other book you own or read?**

Say: **The Bible is special. There are many good books out there. Some are funny or even helpful. But only the Bible is God's Word.**

Got Light?

(The Bible Is

Inspired by God)

Psalm 119:130

Energy Level

Medium Energy

This game will help students articulate how we know the Bible is from God.

Supply List

☐ Bible

☐ one flashlight for each child

The Game

R ead aloud Psalm 119:130. Ask:

• What do you think life would be like without God's Word to direct us?

Ask students to shut their eyes while you turn out the lights and hide your Bible. Have students open their eyes and carefully try to feel around and find the hidden Bible in the dark. After a few moments, give children flashlights and instruct them to try to find the hidden Bible.

Post-Game Discussion Questions

After playing this game, ask your students to form groups of three and discuss:

• What difference did the flashlights make in our game?

• What difference does the Bible make in our lives?

• What does God want you to do with the Bible?

Read aloud Psalm 119:130 once again. Say: **God's words give us hope, direction, and understanding. The Bible tells us about God and how much he loves us. The Bible is inspired by God.**

The Bible Is Absolutely True

(The Bible Is True)

Psalm 119:160

Energy Level

Medium Energy

As you and your kids play a game about what the psalmist said concerning the Bible, your children will discover the Bible is true.

Supply List

- ☐ foam ball or beanbag
- ☐ music
- ☐ Bible

The Game

Gather students together. Have them hold hands and form a circle facing in.

Say: **Sometimes when people tell us things, we wonder if what's said is true. In this game, we won't have to wonder because everyone** *must* **tell the truth while playing it. That's a rule!**

I'll play some music and introduce a small item into the circle that you'll toss back and forth as the music plays. When the music stops, whoever has the item will step into the center of the circle and share one true personal thing. For example, "I'm the youngest person in my family," or "Pizza is my favorite food." Play until everyone has a turn in the middle of the circle or time runs out.

In this game you all shared true things. There wasn't any reason to wonder if people were being honest.

Post-Game Discussion Questions

After playing this game, ask your students to sit down in groups of three and discuss:

• **What did you learn about people that you didn't already know?**

• **How easy or hard was it to come up with something true to share? Why?**

Read aloud Psalm 119:160. Say: **The Bible tells us that all of God's words are true.**

• **How can this truth help us trust God and what he says to us in the Bible?**

Say: **The Bible is true. We can trust everything it says and believe it!**

Presto Change-O Face Change

(The Bible Is Able to Change Lives)

Mark 4:3-20
Energy Level
Low Energy
This simple, quiet game provides a visible example of how the Bible can change lives.

Supply List
☐ Bible

The Game

Have children stand in a circle, shoulder to shoulder, hands behind their backs. Choose one person to be "It." Place "It" in the center of the circle.

"It" has eyes closed while you hand a Bible to someone in the circle. That person should hold the Bible behind his or her back. When "It" opens his or her eyes, the person holding the Bible should begin passing it. Explain that whoever is holding the Bible must change the expression on his or her face until he or she hands it off, then his or her expression returns to "normal."

The Bible should continue to move around, reversing or going one direction, and children's expressions should change as the Bible is passed. "It" tries to guess where the Bible is by watching the faces of the players. When the expression changes, "It" points to the person he or she believes is holding the Bible. When "It" guesses correctly who has the Bible, choose a new person to be "It" and continue the game.

Post-Game Discussion Questions

After playing this game, have the group sit down with you to discuss these questions:

• **How did the person who was "It" know who had the Bible?**

• **In what ways does the Bible change a person's life?**

Say: **The way the Bible changes us isn't magic. It's part of God's way of helping each of us become like Jesus.**

Bushel of Books

(The Bible Is a Collection

of Individual Books)

Luke 24:44

Energy Level

Medium Energy

This game of collecting books will provide the kids a visual demonstration that the Bible is actually a collection of books.

Supply List

❑ large quantity of books
❑ baskets or boxes, one per five to seven kids
❑ Bible

The Game

The object of this game is to collect all the books into baskets. Form children into groups of five to seven children. You may use just one group or many to play this game.

Behind each group, stack at least three books per child. Place the bas-

kets about ten feet away. Each child will take a turn putting a book on his or her head and walking to the basket, then taking the book from his or her head and placing it in the basket. Then he or she will run back to the group, and the next child will take a turn. Add variety by assigning kids different ways to return to the starting line, such as crab walking, hopping, or walking backward. When one group finishes, have those kids help another group collect all their books into a basket.

Post-Game Discussion Questions

When the game is over, ask children to join you for a discussion addressing these questions:

• **Where besides in these baskets can you find a collection of books?**

• **What are the names of some of the books that are collected into one book, the Bible?**

Hold up a Bible. Ask:

• **What are some other names for this collection of books?**

Say: **God wants us to know about him and live a life that honors him. He tells us how in this collection of books called the Bible. It's one totally important book!**

Cozy, Comfy Pet Shuffle

(The Bible Is Comforting)

Romans 15:4

Energy Level

Medium Energy

Have children shuffle through an obstacle course with a furry friend to connect the concept that just as pets can comfort us, so does the Bible.

Supply List

❑ plush stuffed animals, as many toys as groups playing simultaneously

The Game

Set up a round trip obstacle course—as simple or complex as you choose. Ask players to form pairs to move through your course: around chairs, squeezing through a narrow space, crawling under a table, and the like. You'll need as many plush toys as you have pairs.

Say: **Lots of people who have pets say that the pets provide comfort and companionship. You're about to take a difficult trip, and you need the comfort a pet provides.**

Demonstrate the route through the obstacle course, then add the surprise: Each pair will "hug" a furry toy pet between them as they move along. The kids can be back-to-back, arm-to-arm, or use any other configuration—as long as the pet is held between their bodies and kids don't use their hands. At your signal, one or more groups secure their pets between them and navigate the course.

Post-Game Discussion Questions

After playing this game, ask students to discuss:

• **How does spending time with a pet give you comfort?**

• **What else comforts you when you're hurt or sad?**

• **How could the Bible be a comfort to you when you're hurt or sad?**

Say: **One reason God gave us the Bible is to encourage us and give us comfort when we need it. The Bible reminds us that God is always with us!**

Breathe Easy

(The Bible Is One Way

God Speaks to Us)

2 Timothy 3:16-17

Energy Level

Low Energy
This game will help your kids discover that God speaks to us through the Bible.

Supply List

❑ children's Bibles, one for each student

The Game

Say: **Have you ever tried to see how long you could hold your breath? What we're going to do today is kind of like that. But instead of holding your breath, let's see how far you can read something out loud in** one breath.

Pass out a Bible to each student. Help students find 2 Timothy 3:16-17. Explain to students they'll all take a deep breath and then read the verses aloud as far as they can read on one breath. Have everyone do it at the same time. Let them try it a few more times. After they've finished, affirm everyone on a job well done.

Post-Game Discussion Questions

After playing this game, discuss the following questions with your students:

• **What do these verses say about the Bible?**

• **Why is the Bible important?**

• **How does God speak to us through the Bible?**

Say: **God uses the Bible to speak to us about many things. If you want to hear God speak, read the Bible!**

It's in the Bag

(The Bible Is Useful for Making Good Decisions)

Hebrews 4:12
Energy Level
High Energy

As you and your children explore how the Bible is "living and active," you'll discover that the Bible is useful for making good decisions.

Supply List
☐ two trash bags
☐ two sets of seven pictures of living or active things, one of the pictures in each set being a Bible
☐ masking tape

The Game

Before the game, create two parallel masking tape lines on the floor, about five feet from each other. Divide children into two groups. Have each group line up single file behind one of the lines, facing the other line.

Give the first person in each line a trash bag with a set of pictures inside, and have them move behind the other masking tape line across from their group, so they're facing their group members.

Say: **Your job is to think of "living and active" things. When your teammate throws the bag to you, catch it, then call out something living and active that *hasn't* been mentioned before. Then throw the bag back to your teammate, and run across to stand behind him or her. Let's see how long it takes you to get all your team members across.** If your group is very small, have them all work together as one team.

Play several rounds. It gets harder to come up with new items the longer you play!

When groups have finished, ask someone in each group to open the bag. Say: **Inside each bag are things that are living and active. Tell me what you've got in your bags.** Give students a chance to show their pictures.

Post-Game Discussion Questions

After playing this game, ask your students to form groups of three and discuss:

• Why do you think a picture of the Bible was in your bag as a living and active thing?

• What does it mean that the Bible is "living and active"?

• How do you think the Bible can help us make decisions?

• Why should we go to the Bible when we're making decisions?

Say: **The Bible is living and active, and that means that it can help us even today. When we have decisions to make, the Bible can help us know the right thing to do.**

Section 4

Holiday Games

Games for your holiday parties or just for fun!

Sunday Best

(Palm Sunday)

Mark 11:1-11
Energy Level
Medium Energy
This game will help children learn to honor Jesus as king.

Supply List
☐ clean clothing, two each of at least three different items: two coats, two shirts, two pairs of pants, two T-shirts, two sweaters, two robes, and so on
☐ masking tape

The Game

Tell children they'll participate in a dress-up relay. Put clothing in two separate piles at one end of the room, with one of each clothing item per pile. Using masking tape, mark a rectangle on the floor in the middle of the room, and designate it as "Jerusalem." Divide the children into two teams, and have them stand opposite the clothing piles.

Tell children they'll pretend they're in Jerusalem when the people came to honor Jesus. Have each team line up single file in the rectangle, and, at your signal, send the first child in line to run to the team's pile of clothing, pull on one piece of clothing, and "go to Jerusalem."

Back in Jerusalem, the child will take off the clothing item, lay it on the floor, and shout, "Hosanna, Hosanna!" The next child in line will pick it up, dash back to the clothing pile, drop it, and pull on another piece of clothing. The process repeats, with no piece of clothing being used twice until everything has been used once.

If you have a small group, you might want to require that each child puts on two or more items of clothing.

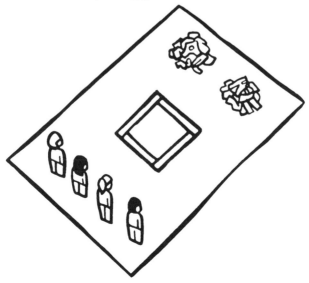

Post-Game Discussion Questions

After playing this game, ask your students to form pairs and discuss:

• What were you feeling as you laid down the clothing and shouted "hosanna"?

• How do you think the people felt who came to see Jesus enter Jerusalem?

• What are some ways we can show honor to King Jesus?

Say: **The people who came to see Jesus were excited! We need to remember that Jesus is still king and deserves our honor and worship.**

Building My Cross

(Good Friday)

John 19:17-18; Romans 6:23

Energy Level

Low Energy

During this game, children will build a cross for themselves and discover Jesus took their place.

Supply List

❑ colored construction paper cut into one-inch strips, approximately twenty strips per child

❑ dice, one die per three or four children

❑ Bible

The Game

Help children form groups of three or four. Give each group one die and twenty strips of paper per child. Ask each group to choose one player to begin the game.

The first player rolls the die and lays the same number of paper strips on the floor, creating a cross that is the same size as the tallest person in the group. The tallest child in each group can lie on the floor and spread out his or her arms to show the group how large to make the cross. The game continues as each player rolls the die and builds the group cross with the paper strips.

When everyone has finished, read aloud Romans 6:23 and John 19:17-18. Then say: **Wow! Because of sin, we all deserve to die. But God loves us so much that he gave Jesus to die in our place on a cross. The gift of God is eternal life!**

Encourage the kids to destroy their crosses—they won't need them! Jesus already made the ultimate sacrifice.

Post-Game Discussion Questions

After playing this game, ask your students to sit down with their groups and discuss:

• **How did you feel as you were building a cross with your group?**

• **What did you feel when you were tearing up your cross? Why do you think you felt that way?**

• **Knowing that Jesus died for you, how do you think you should live your life?**

Say: **Now that you know what Jesus did, Good Friday is a *great* Friday!**

You Can't Keep Jesus Down

(Easter)

Luke 24:1-6
Energy Level

High Energy

Your children will discover that even though people tried to keep Jesus in the grave, they couldn't—just as Jesus said!

Supply List

❑ one large laundry basket, the horizontal kind

❑ five or six helium balloons with *long* strings, able to fit inside the laundry basket

❑ one thick towel or folded blanket, heavy enough to cover the laundry basket and contain the balloons

These supplies are for a group of up to twelve children. If you have a larger group, form them into groups of up to twelve, and give each group the above supplies.

The Game

Before your kids arrive, place the helium balloons inside the laundry basket, and cover them with the towel or blanket.

Say: **On Easter morning, Jesus rose from the dead. Jesus told his disciples that he would rise. Nothing could keep Jesus in the grave!**

Show kids the basket of balloons. Tell them that the basket represents the grave. The towel is the stone. When God rolled the stone away, Jesus left the tomb. As you remove the towel, let the kids see the balloons rise.

The object of the game is for kids to try to get the balloons back into the basket. Each child may only use one hand. Their other hand must be behind their back. Children must work together to capture all the balloons.

Post-Game Discussion Questions

After playing this game, ask your students to form pairs and discuss:

• **It was pretty cool to see the balloons rise. What do you think it was like when Jesus rose from the dead?**

• **If you had been the first person at the tomb, what would you have done? How would you have felt?**

• **How do you feel about Jesus knowing that he rose from the dead?**

Say: **Easter is a time to celebrate Jesus' power!**

Goo Goo Baby Care

(Mother's Day)

Isaiah 66:12b-13

Energy Level

Medium Energy

By pretending to care for a big baby, children will be reminded of all the ways their mothers care for them.

Supply List

❑ large beach towel, sheet, or something similar, one per group

❑ smaller towel, one per group

❑ clothespins (optional), two per group

❑ O-shaped cereal or other suitable food to feed a baby

❑ baby toys (rattle, teething ring, stuffed toy), one per group

The Game

Kids will pretend to care for a baby. Set up supplies in three separate areas as follows: smaller towels and clothespins for "diapering," cereal or other baby food for feeding, and toys to make a cranky baby smile.

Divide children into groups of five. Ask each group for a volunteer to act as the baby—someone *not* wearing a dress. The "baby" will sit on the "baby blanket" (the large towel) while the other players pull the towel to each area for the appropriate activity. Explain that it's not a race, but a game to see how well they can care for the baby.

Each group will visit each baby care area, trying to put on a towel with clothespins (optional) as a diaper; to feed the baby; and to coo and play with the baby and the toy to get the baby to smile. After each group has visited each of the three areas, they'll return to the starting point and "burp" their baby, patting it on the back until it musters a fake burp.

If there's time and desire, change "babies," and play again.

Post-Game Discussion Questions

After playing this game, have students sit down with their groups and discuss these questions:

• **What kinds of baby care did the game leave out?**

• **What are ways your mother takes care of you?**

• **In what ways is God's care for us like our mother's care for us?**

Say: **Most mothers take good care of their children from the time the children are born until the children are grown. They love their children, just as God loves us.**

Matchbox Memorial

(Memorial Day)

Hebrews 12:1-3
Energy Level

Low Energy

This game will help your kids discover that just as a country has national heroes, Christians have heroes of the faith.

Supply List

- ❏ small toy car
- ❏ newsprint taped to wall
- ❏ marker

The Game

Ask students to sit in a circle facing in. Say: **On Memorial Day, Americans remember people who have served in the armed forces. Right now, let's try to remember people in the Bible who** were "soldiers" for God and taught us something about God.

Name one such hero as an example. David, with God's help, was able to defeat Goliath. Ask if anyone can think of another Bible character. Roll the car to a child with his or her hand raised. That person will then share who he or she is thinking of and how that character teaches us something about God. Have children continue rolling the car to each other and taking turns sharing.

As students share Bible characters, write the characters' names and what they teach us about God on the newsprint. Continue until everyone who wants to share has had a turn. If some students are unable to think of Bible characters but you don't want to leave them out, let them know they can share about any person they know or know of who has taught them something about God—our heroes of faith aren't always in the Bible.

Before you play this game, be ready with other names of Bible heroes. Check out Hebrews 11 for ideas.

Post-Game Discussion Questions

After playing this game, discuss the following questions with your students:

• Why should we remember people who have taught us something about God?

• How can remembering those people help us?

• What's one new thing you learned about God from playing this game?

Say: **The Bible tells us that we can find strength to keep following God by remembering the people who have followed God before us. God can teach us things through the lives of others we read about in the Bible, and even through people we know who are following God now.**

Shaving Father

(Father's Day)

Proverbs 1:8

Energy Level

Low Energy

With each stroke of a pretend razor, children will recall loving instructions that both their earthly father and heavenly Father have given to them.

Supply List

☐ mild shaving cream
☐ toy razors or craft sticks, one per group
☐ towels, one per group
☐ wet washcloths or water source for cleanup

The Game

Divide children into groups of four. Say: **In Proverbs it says, "Listen, my son, to your father's instruction and do not for-** sake your mother's teaching." What do you think that means? Affirm all responses. **Wow! God wants you to listen and obey what your dad tells you. It's for your own good.**

Ask each team to choose one person to represent a father. Kids will carefully wrap their towel around "Father's" neck and put shaving cream on his or her face. Give a toy razor or a craft stick to each team.

In order to shave Father, one person on the team must share an instruction—a bit of advice—he or she has heard from his or her father. Be sensitive to children who may not have a father active in their lives; grandfathers, uncles, teachers, and so on will do fine. After a child has shared one instruction, that player uses the razor to remove some shaving cream off of Father's face. Children pass the razor around the group and continue sharing advice and shaving Father until the child is clean.

To continue playing, ask teams to choose another father. You may want to ask children to share guidance they have heard from God, grandfathers, or their mothers.

Post-Game Discussion Questions

After playing this game, ask your students to sit down with their groups and discuss:

• Why does God want you to listen to instructions from your father?

• How easy or difficult is it to obey your father's instructions? Explain.

• What are some instructions that your heavenly Father has given you? Why is it important to obey them?

Say: **It's awesome to know that fathers give good instructions to children they love. You are loved by both your heavenly and earthly fathers!**

Labor Day Lineup

(Labor Day)

Psalm 104:10-23

Energy Level

Low Energy

This silent icebreaker game encourages your kids to think about the value of God's workers in our world.

Supply List

☐ index cards, one per child

☐ pencils, one per child

The Game

Greet your kids warmly, and briefly talk about the purpose of Labor Day—a special day of rest to honor working people. Say: **We all have parents or other adults in our lives who work hard for us and for God.** Explain that you're going to play a game, and no one should talk until the game is over!

Distribute index cards and pencils, one to each child. Ask kids to close their eyes and think of hardworking adults in their lives. Then ask children to each write the job or occupation of a hardworking adult on their note card. For example, you might say something like, "My own mother is a teacher. So I could write 'teacher' on my card." Encourage kids to write with large, clear letters. You may need to remind them: no talking!

Help younger children, and when everyone has finished, have kids stand up and hold their cards where everyone can see them. Say: **Let's see if we can line ourselves up in alphabetical order—according the job or occupation written on our cards.** Explain that jobs like *basketball player* should be toward the front of the line, while *zoologist* would be at the end. Let the children get to work, without talking.

Once your group is in alphabetical order, play the game again. This time have each child write down a job that they think *they'd* like to have someday.

Post-Game Discussion Questions

After playing this game, ask your students to sit down in groups of three and discuss:

• **How do your parents, or other adults, serve God and others in their work?**

• **What jobs can you do to help God and others now?**

• **How does God help us—and the rest of his creation?**

Say: **God is a hard worker who includes us as his co-laborers. God also values rest, so he provides us with opportunities to relax and receive his strength.**

Happy Harvesters

(Thanksgiving)

Ephesians 5:20
Energy Level
Medium Energy

This game will remind children to be thankful for all that God has given them.

Supply List
❑ toy fruits and/or vegetables, one for each pair of children

❑ sturdy disposable plates, one per child

The Game

Help children form pairs. Ask kids to form two lines in the middle of the room with partners facing each other, about an arm's length apart. Make sure there's plenty of space, as the children will be getting farther apart as they play.

Give each child a sturdy disposable plate. Place a toy fruit or vegetable on each plate in one of the lines. One child from each pair should now have a fruit or vegetable. The children must hold their plates with both hands and toss the fruit or vegetable to their partners using only the plates. The partners must try to catch the food on their plates. After they catch it, they should take one small step backward. If a child drops the fruit or vegetable, he or she has to scoop it up with the plate and name one thing he or she is thankful for before tossing it to his or her partner.

The children can bend their plates slightly to make it easier to keep the fruit or vegetable on the plate. You also might want to give the "less round" toy fruits, such as bananas or bunches of grapes or cherries, to the youngest children in the group. These don't slide off as easily as apples!

Post-Game Discussion Questions

After playing this game, ask your students to sit down in groups of three and discuss:

• **How hard or easy was it to think of something you're thankful for in this game? Explain.**

• **How does God provide for us every day?**

• **What are some other things you are thankful for?**

Say: **The Bible tells us that we should always give thanks to God for everything, not just at Thanksgiving time, but every day!**

Preparation Station

(Advent)

Isaiah 40:1-11
Energy Level

Low Energy

This game will help your kids understand what it means to prepare their hearts, minds, and lives for Jesus' coming during Advent season.

Supply List

☐ white board or newsprint, marker

The Game

Ask children to help you brainstorm ways we can prepare our hearts, minds, and lives for Jesus' coming during Advent. You may want to write these ideas on a white board or newsprint for students to refer to later. For example, students might say, "Sing Advent songs," "Read the Bible," or "Pray."

Explain that students will be playing a game about preparing for Jesus' coming. You'll begin the game by saying: "I'm preparing for Christmas, and I'm going to **A**sk God to come into my heart this season." The next person will say the same sentence starter and then complete it with a preparation option that begins with the letter B (for example, "**B**ring a friend to church"). Encourage students to help each other, as some of the letters will be more difficult than others.

Post-Game Discussion Questions

After playing this game, have your students sit down in groups of three and discuss these questions:

• How can you use some of these ideas to help you prepare for Jesus' coming?

• Why does God want us to take time during the season of Advent to prepare for Jesus' coming?

Say: **Advent is such a special time; we can use some of these great ideas to help us prepare our hearts, minds, and lives for Jesus' coming.**

The Waiting Game

(Christmas)

Luke 2:25-33
Energy Level

Low Energy

This icebreaker game will help your kids discover that God delivers on his promises—even when waiting is part of his plan.

Supply List

☐ none needed

The Game

Gather your group together, and ask:

• **How many days are left until Christmas?**

Help kids figure the correct answer, and then say: **Most people think it's hard to wait for Christmas— and for other special events.** Refer to the story of Simeon, and talk about how he waited his entire *life* to meet baby Jesus!

Help your kids divide into groups of three. Say: **We're going to get to know one another better. Please take** turns introducing yourself to your group. Along with sharing your name, I also want you to tell the group about something special you are waiting for—or have waited for in the past. Get them started by introducing yourself. For example, you might say something like, "Hi. I'm Mrs. Martinez, and I waited a long time for my trip to Scotland."

When the groups have finished, gather students into one circle. Ask trios to take turns introducing their members to the whole class. Start them off with a helpful example, such as, "This is Johnny, and he waited a long time to go camping with his dad." Continue until everyone has been introduced.

Post-Game Discussion Questions

Once everyone has been introduced, lead a group discussion using these questions:

• **How does it feel to wait for special days or events? Why?**

• **How do you act when you feel frustrated or impatient?**

• **How did Simeon respond when he finally saw baby Jesus?**

Say: **God often makes us wait for the things we want, but he always delivers the things he promises.**

Wild 'n' Wacky Games

*These games will get your kids up,
moving, and having an over-the-top blast!*

Mummy Wrestling

Exodus 14:13-14
Energy Level
High Energy

This game will help kids realize that we're all helpless without God.

Supply List
❑ two sleeping bags with drawstring tops

❑ masking tape

The Game

This game is best played on a carpeted surface. Use masking tape to create a circle on the floor about six feet in diameter. Clear the area of any obstacles.

Ask for two volunteers to begin the game. They should be approximately the same size. Have these first two players each step inside a sleeping bag. Have them kneel inside the circle. Secure the drawstring of each sleeping bag above the shoulders of each player, with their arms inside the bag. Tell them that the object of the game is for one player to make the other player cross the tape line and go outside the circle. Players can *gently* push, pull, or wrestle, but they must stay inside their sleeping bags and remain kneeling. Observers should cheer on the mummy wrestlers.

Limit each match to about a minute or two. If any part of a player's body or sleeping bag crosses the line, that pair is finished, and two new players take a turn. Be sure opponents are always of approximately equal size and weight. If you have mostly younger kids, make the circle smaller. Let everyone take a turn at mummy wrestling.

Post-Game Discussion Questions

After playing the game, ask your students to sit down in groups of three and discuss:

• **What was it like not being able to use your arms and legs in this game like you usually do? Why?**

• **How is that like trying to fight your battles on your own, without God?**

• **Why is trusting God to help us better than trying to solve problems on our own?**

Encourage kids to always turn to God with their problems. We don't have the tools, information, or power to fight all our battles...but God does!

Music-Moving David

2 Samuel 6:14-15

Energy Level
High Energy
This game will help students demonstrate creative joy in praising God.

Supply List
❑ fast-paced, *current* Christian music
❑ CD or cassette player

The Game

Listen with your kids to the music you provide. After listening to one or two songs together, divide the class into groups of about five. Each person should create one music-inspired move. Then have each small group combine the members' moves for a new creative-movement routine to teach to the other groups. Play the music as they practice.

After all the groups have practiced their new creative movements, call everyone back together again.

As the music plays again, have each group take a turn leading the class in its creation. They should speed up their moves as they go, attempting to get everyone to move faster and faster to the music. Make sure that each group gets a turn.

Post-Game Discussion Questions

After playing this game, ask your students to sit down in their groups. Say: **The Bible tells us that David "danced before the Lord with all his might, while he and the entire house of Israel brought up the ark of the Lord with shouts and the sound of trumpets."**

Have the groups discuss these questions:

• **How do you think God felt when he saw King David dancing with all his might? Why?**

• **What do you think of dancing?**

• **What are some other creative ways we can celebrate and praise God?**

Three for All

Psalm 33:3
Energy Level
High Energy
This game will help kids celebrate the many gifts God has given us that help us adapt in our ever-changing world.

Supply List
❑ playground equipment (various balls, balloons, jump-ropes, Hula hoop plastic hoops, Frisbee flying discs), at least one per person
❑ large open area

The Game

Form your students into two groups facing each other on opposite sides of the play area. The playground equipment should be scattered across the playing field.

In this relay, the first person from each group will choose a piece of playground equipment and start to use it while singing a song and moving toward the other side of the play area. Two children will be crossing the play area at the same time, one from each direction.

As the children are crossing, shout "Joy!" a few times. Every time you shout "Joy!" the children crossing must also shout "Joy!" and then put down the ball or toy they were using and choose a new piece of equipment. Each child must then do something different with this new item while singing a new song and completing his or her journey to the other side of the play area.

When each person arrives at the other side, the next person from that team can repeat the process of crossing the area while singing and using the playground equipment. Continue shouting "Joy!" to have the children respond with "Joy!" and choose new equipment. Continue until both teams have crossed to the other side of the play area. If you have a large group, send two or more players from each team at a time.

Post-Game Discussion Questions

After playing this game, ask your students to sit down in groups of three. Say: **The Bible tells us to "sing to him a new song; play skillfully, and shout for joy"** (Psalm 33:3). Have the groups discuss these questions:

• How did it feel to try to do three different things at once in this game? Explain.

• Why do you think God gave us the ability to do many different tasks at the same time?

• What do you do that gives you joy and makes you want to praise God?

Bonez!

Ezekiel 37:1-14
Energy Level
High Energy

As they play this game, your children will discover that with God there is always hope.

Supply List
☐ none needed

The Game

Say: **Let's play a game that will help us remember the story of Ezekiel and the dry bones.** Inform the children that they are each a "dry bone." Have them mill around the playing area. **Dry bones, hear the word of the Lord. Make a skeleton of __ bones.** (Choose a number between four and ten.)

Have the children form groups of the number you called out, lie on the floor, and organize themselves into the shape of a skeleton. Children can be an arm, a head, a leg, or a torso. If you call out a large number, two or three children can make up a body part. If there are extra "bones" that won't fit into any of the groups that you called, allow them to join into any group they like.

After all the groups have formed their skeletons, have the children stand and begin milling around again. Continue playing as long as time and interest allow.

Post-Game Discussion Questions

After playing a fast-paced game with a large group of children, you might find the children need help calming down. Have them sit down. Make a game of the children taking several slow, deep breaths. After everyone has settled, discuss these questions:

• **How do you think you would feel if you** *really* **saw a bunch of dry bones come to life and join together to form skeletons?**

• **Tell about a time when you were in so much trouble that you thought you'd never get out of it. How did you feel?**

• **How do you think God's people felt when they learned that God would still love and help them even though they did wrong things?**

• **What's the best part of knowing that God loves and helps us—no matter what?**

Say: **It's great to know that God loves us and will always help us, even when we sin!**

Harvest Relay

John 15:16;
Ephesians 5:9
Energy Level
High Energy
The children will each do his or her part in this wacky team game.

Supply List
❑ tough-skinned fruits and/or vegetables (pumpkin, squash, watermelon, cucumber, orange, lemon, and so on), at least one per child
❑ masking tape

The Game

Choose four areas in your play space to serve as four harvest areas, and mark each with masking tape boundaries on the floor. Tell kids these areas represent the field, the basket by the side of the field, the trailer that carries the baskets, and the barn. Place all the fruits and vegetables in the field (the first harvest area). Have kids form three groups and assign them to wait at the "field," the "basket" (the second harvest area), or the "trailer" (the third harvest area).

The goal of the game is to work together to quickly bring in the harvest.

Kids in the field must get all the fruits and vegetables from their area to the basket. They do this by getting on their hands and knees and pushing the fruits and vegetables with their noses or the tops of their heads. (Noses work best for pushing small fruit, heads work best for large vegetables.) Each player pushes one fruit or vegetable at a time and then runs back to the field to see if there's more to harvest. As soon as the first fruits and vegetables start arriving at the basket, kids waiting there will push them to the trailer, also on their hands and knees using their noses and heads. As the fruits and vegetables arrive at the trailer, the third group of kids will push them to the barn, using their noses and foreheads.

Encourage children to hurry with the harvest. Kids will quickly realize that to have a fast harvest, they must look out for one another when pushing and keep at it even when it's hard. Kids may even find ways to help others who are pushing a lopsided vegetable that won't roll straight. When the entire harvest is in the barn, congratulate children for their great work.

Post-Game Discussion Questions

After playing this game, ask your students to sit in small groups and discuss:

• How did we work together to bring in the harvest?

• What kind of fruit do Christians grow?

• What can we do to grow this kind of fruit in our lives?

Say: Jesus said that his followers should grow fruit that lasts. That fruit includes goodness, righteousness, and truth.

Go!

Acts 1:8
Energy Level

High Energy

As they play this running game, children will realize that Jesus wants us to tell the whole world about him.

Supply List

- ❑ masking tape
- ❑ four pieces of paper
- ❑ marker

The Game

Create four parallel lines on the floor using masking tape. Make each line long enough so all your kids can stand on it at one time. Lines must be at least ten feet apart. Use the paper and the marker to make four signs: "Jerusalem," "Judea," "Samaria," and "The ends of the earth." Place each of the signs at one end of each of the tape lines, with "Jerusalem" by the first line, "Judea" next, then "Samaria," and "The ends of

the earth" by the far line.

Say: **Jesus told his disciples to go to Jerusalem, all Judea, Samaria, and the ends of the earth to tell people the good news about him.**

Explain that Jerusalem was the city where Jesus' disciples lived. Judea was the region around Jerusalem, Samaria was a nearby region, and "the ends of the earth" were far off countries that had never heard about Jesus.

Say: **Let's pretend that you're Jesus' disciples, because you are! I'll call out "Jerusalem," "Judea," "Samaria," and "ends of the earth." When you hear me, run to whichever tape line I called.** Show children the tape lines you've labeled. **When the whole missionary team arrives, then everyone should count to three and shout, "Jesus loves you!" all together.**

Have the children stand on the Jerusalem line to begin the game. As you shout out new locations for the children to run to, be sensitive to the speed of the slowest children. Don't rush the pace of the game so that some kids are being left behind. Remember that they are a missionary *team*. Play as long as time, interest, and energy allow.

Post-Game Discussion Questions

After playing this game, have the children sit down in groups of four and discuss:

• How did it feel to do so much traveling to announce that Jesus loves us? Explain.

• How do you think Jesus' friends felt when Jesus told them to tell the whole world about him? Explain.

• Who are some people that you can share Jesus with?

• What are some ways that we can help missionaries with their job of reaching "the ends of the earth"?

Say: Jesus wants his followers to tell the whole world about him. We can start at home, but let's try to help our missionaries, too.

Indoor Olympics

1 Corinthians 9:24-27

Energy Level

High Energy

This game will test kids' skill as they participate in wacky olympic games. Remind kids that the Bible says that life is like a race with an eternal prize.

Supply List

❑ masking tape

❑ one box of plastic straws

❑ paper plates, one for every four students if you're having kids rotate through the four areas. If you'll have all kids play each game at the same time, you'll need one plate per child.

❑ crepe paper streamers, two for every four students if you're having kids rotate through the four areas. If you'll have all kids play each game at the same time, you'll need two streamers per child.

The Game

Before class, set up the following game stations in your play area. A large area works best. Use masking tape to make a starting line at each station.

At the *javelin throwing* station, set out a supply of plastic drinking straws. Kids will see how far they can throw the straws. At the *discus tossing* station, set out a supply of paper plates. Kids will see how far they can toss the plates. At the *slalom* station, create an obstacle course by setting chairs, trash cans, and other classroom objects in such a way that kids can weave in and around them. Kids will relay race through the course. At the *synchronized swimming* station, set out a supply of crepe paper streamers and make a masking tape line about twenty feet from the starting line. Group members will together "swim" to the tape line and back, waving their streamers artistically.

Help kids form four groups, and let each group make up a fictitious country to represent. Kids can create flags, mottos, and anthems for their countries if you have time. Explain the four different stations. Have each group go to a different station and, at your signal, participate in that sport. You may want to have an adult at each station to explain the rules, cheer kids on, and do the judging.

After all the groups have been to all the stations, lead kids in applause for everyone's participation.

Post-Game Discussion Questions

After playing the game, ask your students to sit down in groups of three and discuss:

• **What was it like to participate in these olympic games? Why?**

• **What do real Olympic athletes have to do to win their events?**

• **What can you do to discipline yourself to run the race of life in a way that pleases God?**

Explain that reading the Bible, praying, and obeying Jesus will help kids to always be winners!

Uppies and Downies

2 Corinthians 4:8

Energy Level

High Energy

This game will help your kids discover that God never abandons them in hard times, but helps them get up and keep going.

Supply List

❑ masking tape

❑ ten to fifteen rubber safety cones

If you don't have cones, call your local schools' physical education departments, the city recreation department, or a construction company. They are often willing to lend these for classroom use. If you can't find safety cones, substitute something else that's easy to stand up and knock down, such as wooden blocks or cardboard play "bricks."

The Game

Designate side and end boundaries in whatever space you have by putting masking tape on the floor, and clear all obstacles. Set up rubber cones randomly within the play area, and divide your group into two teams of equal size. One group is the Uppies and the other is the Downies. On your signal, the Downies should go around and knock over the cones. The Uppies should race around setting them back up. The two teams can't touch!

After several minutes, call time and have everyone stop. Then have the teams change jobs and play again.

Post-Game Discussion Questions

After playing this game, ask your students to sit down in groups of three and discuss:

• **What did it feel like to have your cones constantly knocked over? Why?**

• **How is that like life sometimes?**

• **How does it feel to know that nothing can keep you down when you have God on your side?**

Say: **We all experience ups and downs in life, but the Bible assures us that nothing can keep us down when we have God on our side!**

Greased Pig

Hebrews 10:23
Energy Level
High Energy

In this wild 'n' wacky game, students will learn what it means to "hold unswervingly" to God's promises.

Supply List
❑ one foam football per twelve kids

❑ a can of vegetable shortening or a bottle of baby oil

❑ a roll of paper towels

The Game

This game will be messy, so encourage students beforehand to dress in play clothes, and secure an outdoor location for game play. Greet children as they arrive, and ask them to "grease up" using vegetable shortening and/or baby oil to make their hands slick. Give the same treatment to a foam football to make catching the ball especially tricky.

Ask the children to form a large circle and pass the ball around and across the circle, counting tosses to see how long they can keep the ball in the air without dropping it. Play several rounds so that everyone has plenty of opportunities to try their slippery hand at the ball. You may want to have rags and a bucket of soapy water on hand for easy cleanup. For larger groups, play with more than one slimy football.

Post-Game Discussion Questions

After playing this game and cleaning up, have the children sit down together. Say: **The Bible tells us to "hold unswervingly to the hope we profess, for he who promised is faithful"** (Hebrews 10:23). Discuss these questions:

• **Why was it hard to hold onto the football in this game?**

• **What things in life make it difficult to hold onto hope?**

• **Why is it sometimes hard to remember what God has in store for us?**

• **Why can we hold unswervingly to the hope God gives us?**

Close by reminding kids to hang on tight to God's promises and not drop the ball when trouble comes.

Building the House

1 Peter 2:4-5
Energy Level
High Energy
Children will work together to build a wall out of shoes and discover they need to work together to be the church.

Supply List
☐ masking tape

The Game

Use the masking tape to mark two parallel starting lines on the floor at least thirty feet apart. Make a masking tape X halfway between the two lines.

Gather the children around you. Say: **The Bible tells us that all of Jesus' friends are like living stones. God wants us to work together to build a strong house. When God's friends join together and cooperate, we are like a special building for God. Let's play a game that will help us understand.**

Divide your class into two work crews. Have each work crew line up behind one of the starting lines so the crews are facing each other. If you have an extra large group, simply add more "work crews." You can have work crews approach the wall from all directions. The more the merrier!

Say: **Your work crews are going to work together to build one big wall out of your shoes. When I say "go," the first person in each line will run to the X, take off his or her shoes, and place them on the X. When those people get back behind their tape line, the next person in the work crew can add his or her shoes to the pile to help build the**

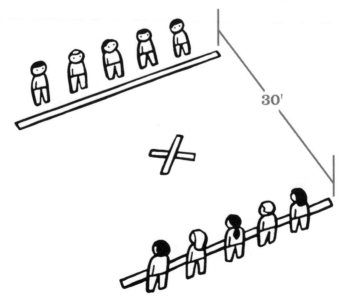

30'

wall. You'll have to work together to make the pile of shoes look something like a wall.

Shout "go!" and let the children start building. Play until all the children have had a turn and are out of shoes.

If you're playing this game at an overnighter or retreat, have children use their sleeping bags as stones instead of their shoes.

Post-Game Discussion Questions

After playing this game, gather the children in a circle around the wall they created. Discuss these questions:

• **What was challenging about building this wall?**

• **How was working together on the wall like working together to be God's family?**

• **Why do you think it's important to God that we work together?**

Say: **God wants us to work together to be the church. He wants us to work close to each other—like stones fitted together in a wall. One of the great things about God's plan is that we get to work close to other people and maybe make new friends!**

Section 6

Total Silence Games

Shhhh! These games are played in absolute silence.
Use them when your kids want to play—
and you need a break!

Mystery Art

Proverbs 3:5

Energy Level

Low Energy

This silent game will teach students to trust God with their lives because God knows what's best.

Supply List

❑ poster board, one sheet for each team of five or six

❑ markers or crayons, one set for each team

The Game

Help students form groups of five or six. Ask each group to choose one person as its leader. Give each group a piece of poster board and markers or crayons, and explain that each team will draw a mystery picture on its poster.

Gather group leaders together, and explain that each leader must choose what object his or her group will draw. Have each group leader quietly tell you what his or her team will draw. Write down the ideas for later reference. Before leaders return to their groups, explain these rules to the entire class:

• The leader of the group may not touch the poster or write anything.

• There will be absolutely no talking.

• Every member of the team—except for the leader—must add something to the picture.

The challenge is for the leaders to direct the project without speaking or writing. Send the leaders back to their groups, and let the game begin. When all the groups have finished, reveal to each group what they were drawing, and see if their pictures are at all recognizable!

Post-Game Discussion Questions

After playing this game, have children form groups of three. Each group should include people from three different drawing teams. Read aloud Proverbs 3:5: "Trust in the Lord with all your heart and lean not on your own understanding." Then have the groups discuss these questions:

• **How was the game we just played like the verse I just read?**

• What was hardest about following your leader's plan for the picture? What was easiest? Explain.

• What's hardest about following God's plan? What's easiest?

• Why should we trust God?

Say: **God is the only one who knows the master plan for our lives, much like your team leaders were the only ones who knew what you were drawing.** Challenge students to trust God even when they aren't sure how things will turn out. God knows best.

Quiet Action

Ecclesiastes 3:7; John 13:35

Energy Level

Medium Energy

This silent game will teach kids to focus on the impact of actions versus words.

Supply List

❑ index cards, each listing the name of a famous biblical character known for some special deed (for example, Eve, Noah, Joseph, Moses, David, Esther, Daniel, Mary, or Peter), one per child

The Game

In this silent version of charades, begin by giving half the class index cards naming famous biblical characters. Instruct them to read their cards silently and not show the cards to anyone. Kids should then act as the person named on their card, without speaking. As soon as any child without a card thinks he or she knows who someone is acting like, he or she will quietly join that child in acting like that character to help the others figure out and join them.

After a few minutes, collect the used cards from the first group of actors. Distribute the remaining cards to the children that did not begin with a card. Now the first group of children must quietly watch the second group act and try to silently join in with at least one person. If you have time, play several rounds, shuffling and redistributing the cards each time. Whether acting or guessing the biblical characters, remind students that no one may talk during the game. The students will not know which characters they guessed correctly until everyone shares the name on his or her card during the discussion.

Post-Game Discussion Questions

After playing this game, ask your students to share the names of the people they were portraying. Then have the students sit down in groups of four or five. Say: **The Bible tells us that there is "a time to be silent and a time to speak"** (Ecclesiastes 3:7). Have students discuss these questions in their groups:

• **How did you know who some of the biblical characters were?**

• **Why do we remember what people do more than what they say?**

• **Why are our actions as Christians important to people who watch us?**

Say: **Jesus said that people will know we are Christians by our love, and that means by our actions.**

Silent Excitement

Luke 19:37-40

Energy Level

High Energy

As your kids explore the story of Jesus' triumphal entry into Jerusalem by playing this game, your kids discover what it means to be excited about Jesus.

Supply List

☐ none needed

The Game

Divide students into two groups, and have the groups stand facing each other. Explain that you have a challenge for them: to show the other group excitement, but totally *silent* excitement. Kids can wave their arms, open their mouths like they're yelling, jump around—anything they want to do that shows excitement, so long as they're silent.

Have groups watch you for the signal to start. When you point to a group, they should show "silent excitement." When you point to the other group, the first team can stop. Whenever you point to either group, they have to show "silent excitement" again. You can make it more fun by switching back and forth quickly to see how quickly the children respond. But remember: They can't laugh or make any noise!

After a few minutes, stop and let both groups know they did a great job with their demonstrations.

Post-Game Discussion Questions

After playing this game, ask your students to sit down in their groups and discuss:

• What made this game difficult? What made it easy?

• Jesus said that if his followers were to keep quiet, "the stones will cry out" (Luke 19:40). What do you think that means?

• When have you been so excited you just couldn't keep quiet?

• What about Jesus makes you really excited?

• How can we help others get excited about what Jesus has done for us?

Say: **Jesus' followers just couldn't keep quiet about him. They had to share their happiness and excitement that Jesus is our Savior. That's something to get excited about! Let's share our joy with others!**

How to Produce Fruit

John 15:1-7
Energy Level
Low Energy

This game will help your kids understand the concept that no branch can bear fruit by itself, but only through Jesus Christ.

Supply List
☐ one quarter
☐ two oranges or other fruit
☐ two craft sticks or tongue depressors

The Game

This totally silent game works well in large groups. Divide kids into two teams. Have them sit down in parallel lines facing each other. Place two craft sticks and two pieces of fruit on the floor between the two teams, near the far end of the lines. Each player must hold hands with the people on either side, and everyone except the first person in each line should close his or her eyes.

Flip a coin at the beginning of the lines for the leaders of each team. Explain that if the coin lands on heads, they should squeeze the next person's hand *once*. The team must pass the signal along the line without speaking. When the last person in line receives the signal, that person should open his or her eyes and pick up *the stick.* If the coin lands on tails, the leader should squeeze the next person's hand *twice.* Again, the team must silently pass the signal down the line. When the last person in line receives the signal, that person should open his or her eyes and pick up *the fruit.* The object of the game is to pick up the correct object as quickly as possible.

Repeat the game several times, seeing if teams can improve their speed. After each round, have the first people in line go to the end, so that you always have a new leader. Remind kids to always keep their eyes and mouths closed, unless they are the first person in line or the last.

Post-Game Discussion Questions

After playing this game, ask your students to sit down in groups of three and discuss:

• Why was it important to be patient in this game?

• Why was it important to pass on the correct signal?

Say: **Jesus told his disciples, "I am the vine; you are the branches. If a man remains in me and I in him, he will bear much fruit; apart from me you can do nothing"** (John 15:5). Ask:

• How is this verse like the game we just played?

• What kind of fruit do you want to produce?

Synchronized Skating

1 Corinthians 8:3
Energy Level
High Energy
This game reminds kids that God knows their every thought and action.

Supply List
☐ paper plates, two per child

The Game

Give each child two paper plates to use as skates. Children place one foot on each plate. Then, kids slide their plates along the floor in an ice-skating motion. Allow a few minutes of "free skating" around the room so that everyone understands how to paper plate skate. Because this is a silent game, remind the children not to say anything while they're practicing.

When the children are comfortable with their "skates," have them form pairs. Explain that the object of the game is to "know" their partners. Without using words or sounds, partners should skate together, trying to do the same moves. They must use eye contact and body movements to give clues to each other in order to skate together as a team. Their knowledge of their partners will help the kids synchronize their skating. Change partners every two minutes in order to allow the kids a chance to know other children in the group.

Post-Game Discussion Questions

After playing this game, ask your students to sit down in groups of three and discuss:

• **As you skated with your partner, did you learn to "know" him or her better? Explain.**

• **How does it make you feel when you realize that if you love God, you are known by him? Why?**

• **How can you stay synchronized with God?**

Say: **Isn't it amazing to realize that God knows you personally? Awesome!**

Show Your Fruit

Galatians 5:22-23
Energy Level
Medium Energy

This game will help your kids understand that they can show by their actions that the Holy Spirit lives in them.

Supply List
☐ Bible
☐ white board or newsprint
☐ markers

The Game

Have students sit in a circle. Have a volunteer read aloud Galatians 5:22-23. Have the group repeat the verses aloud together several times so that students begin to memorize the Scripture. Write the words of the verses on a white board or newsprint so students can see them.

Explain that you'd like the group to create its own signs to show each "fruit." For example, for love, the sign might be crossing arms over the chest. Give the group a few minutes to discuss and create signs, and then go through the signs a few times to make sure everyone knows them.

Then explain how the game will work. One person will stand in the middle of the circle and spin around. When he or she stops spinning, he or she will point at one person in the circle. That person will immediately make one of the signs. The people on either side of that person need to immediately determine which signs should be before or after the sign that person has made and then make those signs as quickly as they can. For example, if the person pointed to makes the sign for *joy*, the students on either side should make the signs for *love* and *peace*. After the signs have been made, have the person who was pointed to take a turn in the middle. Continue in this manner until everyone has had a turn in the middle.

Remind students to remain silent for the entire game.

Post-Game Discussion Questions

After playing this game, have the students discuss these questions:

• What was it like to make these signs for the fruit of the Spirit? Why?

• What are some other ways you can show the fruit of the Spirit in your own life?

Say: **The fruit of the Spirit is what shows in our lives when we have God in our hearts. God wants us to show these things to everyone we meet.**

Hush Hush Bubble Rush

Galatians 6:9
Energy Level

Medium Energy

This game teaches persistence as it challenges players to propel bubbles across the room while keeping quiet.

Supply List

❑ bubble solution, one container per four kids

❑ bubble wands, one per four kids

❑ cardboard pieces or homemade paper fans

❑ masking tape

The Game

Mark two lines on the floor with masking tape, far enough apart so that it will be moderately difficult to get bubbles moved from the start to the finish line. Divide kids into clusters of three or four, and have them begin at the starting line. One child in each group should blow some bubbles; the others use their hands, cardboard, fans, whatever they choose to move the bubbles across the finish line. Set a time limit, such as forty-five seconds. Nobody may speak during the game. Observe how children work together to accomplish the task.

Post-Game Discussion Questions

After playing this game, ask the children to sit down and talk about the game, using these discussion questions:

• **What was hard or easy about this game? Explain.**

• **How did you feel when it was difficult to get the bubbles across the finish line?**

• **When are some other times you feel that way? What are some good things you try to do but sometimes are so difficult that you feel like quitting?**

Say: **Some good things we do are worth doing, even if they're hard and we get tired. God promises that when we keep working to do what's right, he'll reward us.**

A-mazing Concentration

Philippians 3:17

Energy Level

Medium Energy

This game will help demonstrate the value of Christian teamwork to achieve a goal.

Supply List

☐ sixteen paper plates (or pieces of construction paper), eight lightly marked "Yes" and eight lightly marked "No" on the back so that students can't see the words from the front

The Game

Put the plates (or paper) on the floor in a 4x4-foot grid so that the plain sides face up. Have students take turns flipping over a plate to see what's underneath. If the plate says "Yes," that student can step on that plate and try again to find another "Yes" to walk on, finding a path through the plates. If a plate says "No," that student's turn is over and he or she turns over all the "Yes" plates for the next student to try.

Students watching can give non-verbal clues to help their friends get through the maze as quickly as possible, with everyone on the team required to find and step on all eight "Yes" plates after a teammate finds them all. The object of this game is to find all eight "Yes" plates and have everyone on the team turn them over and step on them in the same exact pattern, getting through the "maze."

Post-Game Discussion Questions

After playing this game, ask your students to sit down. Read aloud Philippians 3:17: **"Join with others in following my example, brothers, and take note of those who live according to the pattern we gave you."** Have the students discuss these questions:

• **How long would this game have taken if you were playing alone? Why?**

• **Why did you need your friends to help you?**

• **What are some ways we help each other find the right way to follow God?**

Silent Lineup

Colossians 3:11

Energy Level

Medium Energy

In this game, children arrange themselves in different orders depending on characteristics you choose. Through the variety of different characteristics, they can recognize that through their many differences, they all are members of God's family.

Supply List

❑ none needed

The Game

Form children into groups of ten to twelve. If you have a small class, they can play the game all together. When you name a characteristic, such as age, the children have to arrange themselves in a line based on that characteristic (for example, youngest to oldest or vice versa). No talking or whispering is allowed. Kids may use sign language, gestures, and nonverbal expressions. Play the game several times, using different characteristics each time, such as age, hair length, shoe size, height, or number of buttons on their shirts.

Post-Game Discussion Questions

After playing this game, have the children sit down and discuss these questions:

• **How did you know how to arrange your group, since you couldn't talk?**

• **In what ways are some of you the same?**

• **What kinds of things do you all have in common, even though you are different ages, from different families, and so on?**

Say: **With all our differences, from our looks and abilities to our names and family histories, we all can share the privilege of being part of God's family.**

Silent Instruction

1 Thessalonians 4:11

Energy Level

Medium Energy

This game will help your kids discover that it's possible to follow instructions without hearing a word—just as it's possible to follow God without physically hearing his voice.

Supply List

❑ food items and utensils to make a sandwich

❑ several new toothbrushes and toothpaste

❑ clean items of clothing such as socks and hats

The Game

Students will choose partners to complete a task without saying a word. You, the leader, will whisper an unusual request to one person in each pair (for example, make a toothpaste sandwich, put socks on your head, put hats on your feet, or brush your teeth with jelly). Give each pair the same assignment, and whisper so no other pair gets an unfair advantage! The student who listened to your instructions can only nod or shake his or her head as his or her partner, without speaking, tries to point or use signals to figure out and do the task you whispered. After a pair finishes one task, partners switch roles and you whisper new instructions so they can complete a different task. Any pair that finishes both tasks joins another pair. These helpers give nonverbal clues to help another pair finish.

Post-Game Discussion Questions

After playing this game, have the children sit down in groups of four and discuss these questions:

• **How did you know what your partner wanted you to do?**

• **How do you know what God wants you to do?**

• **How does living a quiet life help us focus on following God?**

Say: **Following God requires intense concentration. Just as you had to focus on your partner to do your task, you must focus on God to understand what he wants you to do.**

Section 7

Travel Time Games

*Ten games to play when you're on
your way from here to there.*

Travel Word Search

Joshua 1:8

Energy Level

Low Energy

This game will provide a fun thinking activity for children as they travel. It will also keep their focus on Jesus and the Christian life.

Supply List

☐ none needed

The Game

Help children agree on a "religious" word to spell. Some examples may include *Jesus*, *disciple*, *promises*, *Bible*, *parable*, *miracle*, and so on. As you travel, ask children to look at signs and billboards along the road for the letters to spell the selected word. The letters do not have to be the first letter of a word on a sign, and they can use more than one letter on a particular sign. But, the letters to the selected word must be found *in order*! Once a word has been completed, ask children to select a new word to spell.

To make this game more challenging, use the following variation. Rather than looking for letters, children will search the signs and scenery for things that start with the letters to spell the selected word. For example, to spell *Christian*, children might point out a cow, a horse, a restaurant, ice, a store, a tree, the interstate, an airplane, and a napping passenger. Once again, the letters must be found in order. Encourage children to be creative and have fun!

Post-Game Discussion Questions

After playing this game, use the following questions to guide a discussion with the children.

• **What things did you see that God made?**

• **Which of the words that we spelled is your favorite? Why is that word special to you?**

• **Joshua 1:8 tells us to think about God's Word day and night. How has this game helped you think about God?**

Say: **Everywhere you look, you can see God at work!**

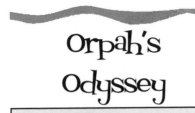

Orpah's Odyssey

Ruth 1:14

Energy Level

Low Energy

This game will help students re-enact Ruth's persistence and Orpah's change of direction.

Supply List

☐ none needed

The Game

One student will name an object he or she has just seen and then list at least three items that match that object. For example, if a student says "car," he could add brands like "Ford," parts like "tires," or colors like "red." If the student names something like "oak tree," she could name "acorns, leaves, maple tree" to go with the first item.

After naming at least three matches to the first object, anyone else can say "Ruth" and then continue adding to that person's list, or "Orpah" and then start a new list of his or her own. The easy version of the game—if you have monotonous scenery—is to allow students to name any item that matches the first object without necessarily being able to see it. If you want to challenge your students, require them to look out the window or in the vehicle and actually see the matching items they name that go with the first item mentioned.

Post-Game Discussion Questions

After playing this game, remind students that Ruth stayed with her mother-in-law, while Orpah returned to her homeland. Ask your students to discuss these questions:

• **Which was harder, playing as Ruth or Orpah? Why?**

• **Why did Orpah decide to go home instead of following Naomi to a new country?**

• **Why did Ruth decide to follow Naomi to a new country instead of going home?**

Say: **We can travel anywhere, knowing that God goes with us and helps see us through new experiences.**

Name That Joyful Song

Psalm 100:1-2
Energy Level

Medium Energy

Time will fly as kids use their imaginations to re-create worship songs for everyone in the vehicle to guess. Then, join in the fun as everyone plays and sings the song together.

Supply List

❑ empty plastic water or soda bottles, one per person

The Game

Encourage everyone to grab an empty water or soda bottle to participate in the fun. Choose one person to lead the game by using his or her bottle as an instrument. The leader either blows across his or her bottle or taps on the vehicle seat to play part of a worship song. Everyone listens and tries to guess the name of the song. Then, when the song is revealed, all join in playing and singing the worship song together.

Players may want to name a category before they begin playing their song. For example, children's church song, contemporary Christian song from the radio, hymn, youth group song, praise team song, choir song, and so on.

Post-Game Discussion Questions

After playing this game, ask your students to discuss these questions:

• **What do you think the Bible means when it says to "come before him with joyful songs"?**

• **How does it make you feel when you sing joyful songs to God? How do you think God feels?**

• **Where can you sing joyful songs to God?**

Say: **It's nice to think that we may have made God glad by singing joyful songs to him today.**

Spin a Yarn

Psalm 133:1

Energy Level

Low Energy

Sharing with one another promotes unity, so find out what everyone is thinking and feeling—or just have fun telling stories—and keep the peace on a long road trip!

Supply List

❑ ball of yarn made from scraps of many different lengths and colors of yarn tied together. Make sure you vary the lengths of yarn, with some very long and several very short pieces. Making the ball of yarn would be a good road-trip project in itself!

The Game

Decide on a topic or use an idea from the list below. One person begins by winding yarn from the ball into a new ball while talking about the chosen topic. When he or she gets to the first knot, he or she stops talking and passes both balls to the next person.

That person continues winding the new ball while speaking on the topic until he or she reaches the next knot. Continue until the last piece of yarn is reached or everyone has had a turn. If the yarn runs out before everyone has had a turn on a particular topic, or you just want to continue playing, simply begin again making a new ball, starting at the end of yarn you just finished with.

Topic suggestions:

• Describe something that you (or others in the vehicle) are really good at.

• Talk about good things about the person on your right.

• Talk about ways you've seen God work in your life.

• Name the two most important people in your life, besides your parents, and tell why you chose them.

• Describe the best [or worst] thing that happened to you today [this week, in your life].

• Tell a Bible story, pausing at the knots and passing the balls to the next person to continue. The story cannot end until someone reaches the end of the string.

• Retell a Bible story with modern characters and setting.

• Talk about expectations, hopes, and dreams for the trip you're on.

Post-Game Discussion Questions

After playing this game, discuss:

• Was it easy or hard to get along with everyone during this game? Explain.

• How did it feel to have everyone listen when you talked?

• Did you learn anything new about someone? Explain.

Say: **We just experienced Psalm 133:1, "How good and pleasant it is when brothers [friends] live [ride] together in unity!"**

Funny Questions

Matthew 7:7

Energy Level

Low Energy

This game will help your kids discover that they can ask God anything as they get to know each other by asking questions.

Supply List

❑ index cards with questions written on them (see below)

The Game

Before you go on your trip, write these questions on index cards, one question per card, and have them nearby while you're traveling. Feel free to add others of your own.

• What food would you most like to smear on a wall, and why?

• If you could live anywhere, where would you choose?

• If your parents let you choose your own meals for one whole day, what would you eat?

• What color would you most like to dye your hair, and why?

• What's the strangest dream you've ever had?

• If you could have any animal as a pet, what would it be?

• What's one rule in your home that you don't like, and why?

• If you were given three wishes, what would you wish for, and why?

• If you could be anything, what would you like to be when you grow up?

While you're traveling together, ask students to play a game with you.

Say: **I'm going start by asking a silly question, and you take turns answering it. Then, someone else can ask a silly question and everyone can answer that one, too. If you can't think of a silly question, I've got some you can use.**

Have a question ready or use one of the above questions. Be sure to remove an index card after you use it. Give everyone who wants to a turn to respond. Then ask the next person to think of a silly question, or if that person can't think of one, he or she can use one from your index cards and ask it to the group. Let everyone respond. Do this until you run out of questions to ask or until you're almost at your destination.

Post-Game Discussion Questions

After playing this game, discuss the following questions with your students:

• What's one new thing you learned about someone just now?

• Have you ever asked God a question and got an answer? Tell about that experience.

• What do you think God feels when we ask him questions?

Say: **The Bible says that if we ask, it's ours...if we look, we'll find...and if we knock, the door will be opened. God loves it when we ask him questions!**

Word Play

John 1:1

Energy Level

Low Energy

This travel game will get kids thinking about how God has spoken to us through Jesus.

Supply List

❏ paper and pencils for all participants

❏ Bible

The Game

When everyone is snugly bundled into the vehicle, distribute paper and pencils to anyone who wants to participate in some playful "mad-libs." First, ask children to use the paper and pencils to rewrite a familiar children's story or fairy tale. Offer suggestions of simple common stories, such as: *Goldilocks and the Three Bears*, *The Three Little Pigs*, or *Little Red Riding Hood*.

When the children have finished writing their stories, talk them through the next step. Say: **Now underline several of the words. Underneath, write what kind of word you've underlined—a place, a thing, an action, a person's name, an animal...Then erase the word you first wrote, leaving only the blank space and the description.**

If another adult sponsor is available, ask him or her to offer help as needed with this complicated step and collecting the mad-libs. Otherwise assign the task to an older, helpful student. In an orderly way, ask children to suggest the words as the assigned helper fills in the blanks. Keep in mind that if a word is used more than once throughout a story (such as a key person or animal), the helper may need to substitute the new word each time so the story makes sense.

When all the blanks have been filled, and all the stories are completed, have the children read the zany tales aloud for laughs.

Post-Game Discussion Questions

After playing this game, ask for a volunteer to read aloud John 1:1. Then discuss these questions:

• **How important was each word in these stories?**

• **How is Jesus like God's "word" to us?**

• **What story did Jesus tell us about God?**

• **How does Jesus help us understand what God is like?**

Give this game a go on your next endless road trip, and let the good times roll!

What's That You Say?

Acts 2:1-12

Energy Level

Low Energy

This game will remind kids of how God caused the disciples to speak in different languages on the day of Pentecost.

Supply List

☐ none needed

The Game

Play a guessing game with kids as you travel. Explain that you'll start by saying a sentence, and kids will have to try to guess the secret of the sentence. Say that the secret is a certain pattern of speech.

Make up a sentence about packing for a trip in which your name and the first thing you're packing both begin with the same letter. For example, if your name is Nancy, you might say, "My name is Nancy, and I'm packing my nightgown, my jeans, and my hat."

(Kids might think that the trick is that you're naming things to wear.)

Then let the next person say a similar sentence, stating his or her name and what he or she is packing. See if the person has caught on to your speech pattern. If so, congratulate him or her, and continue playing until all the children have figured out the pattern. Then play again, making up another speech pattern to follow.

Post-Game Discussion Questions

After playing the game, ask your students to discuss:

• **Was it easy or hard to try to figure out my speech pattern in this game? Why?**

• **How do you think the people felt on the day of Pentecost when everyone was speaking in different languages? Explain.**

• **What can you do to make sure you have better communication with your family members and friends?**

Remind kids that God made the disciples speak in different languages at Pentecost so that all the people visiting could hear about Jesus in their own languages. How can your kids tell others about Jesus?

Talent Rhythm

1 Corinthians 3:6-9
Energy Level
Medium Energy
Children will discover different ways they can serve the church while they keep a driving beat.

Supply List
☐ none needed

The Game

Instruct the children to each choose one word to describe a talent that they can use to serve the church. For example, a child might say, "Paint," "Sing," "Give," "Clean," or "Read." Make sure that no two children choose the same word. Have the children take turns saying their words out loud. This will help all the children remember the words.

Say: **Let's play a rhythm game that will help us remember that there are many ways to serve the church. Let's practice the rhythm first.**

Instruct the children to pat their legs twice and then snap their fingers twice. Tap a steady rhythm on the steering wheel to help the children keep cadence. Instruct the children to repeat the sequence over and over.

Stop the children, and say: **Good job. Now we're going to add one more thing. I'll choose one child to start the game. That child will say his or her talent on the first pat, and someone else's talent at the second pat. If you hear your talent called, then you are now "It." When the rhythm returns to the leg patting, it's your turn to say your talent and then someone else's talent. Let's see how long we can keep the rhythm going.**

Help the children start the rhythm again. Choose a child to begin. Let the rhythm continue until a child is unable to continue it. Start the game over, and allow the child who ended the last rhythm to start this one.

Post-Game Discussion Questions

After the children have played several rounds, have them discuss these questions:

• **Why do you think God gives people different gifts?**

• **What kinds of things could this carload of kids do for God if you worked together?**

• **What should we do first? When should we do it?**

Freeze!

Ephesians 5:16

Energy Level
Low Energy
Children will play a fun traveling game and discover that we need to use our time well.

Supply List
☐ pencils, one per child
☐ paper for each child
☐ vehicle's CD player, tape player, or radio

The Game

Ask a child to help you out by giving each child some paper and a pencil. Say: **Let's play a thinking game. When I start the music, start writing down as many ideas as you can about things you can do for God in one day. See if you can get twenty different ideas written down. You might write that you could read the Bible or share something. Keep writing down ideas until you hear the music stop.**

Start the music and let it play for a minute or two. Stop the music in the middle of a song. Say: **Time's up!** Ask:
• **How did you do?**

Say: **Let's try again, and this time I'll give you a different category. This time write down twenty things that you'd like to do for God this** *year.* Repeat the game, stopping the music midsong.

Let's play one last time. This time write down twenty things that you would like to do for God during your *lifetime.* Repeat the game, stopping the music midsong.

Post-Game Discussion Questions
After playing this game, have the children discuss these questions:
• **How did it feel not knowing how much time you had to finish writing your list?**
• **How is that like real life?**
• **Why is it important to use our time well to serve God?**

Say: **We don't know how much time we have to serve God. So we need to make the most of our time. By living in a way that makes God happy, we can use our time well—no matter what we're doing.**

What's on Your Mind?

Philippians 4:8-9

Energy Level

Low Energy

This game will help your kids understand that they can find good things in the world around them if they only choose to look for them.

Supply List

☐ Bible

The Game

Have a volunteer read aloud Philippians 4:8-9. Explain that your kids will be doing a mobile scavenger hunt to find things that would fit into the cate-gories listed in this verse. For example, they might see someone helping a stranded motorist or a sign advertising a church. Challenge the group to find as many things as they can during your trip, and make sure that all members of the group agree that the chosen items fit into the categories.

Post-Game Discussion Questions

After playing this game, have the students discuss these questions:

• Was it easy or difficult to find things to fit into these categories? Explain.

• How can you show these things in your own life?

Say: It sometimes seems like there's nothing good in the world. But as you saw in this game, there's good all around us if we just look for it. God wants us to focus on good things such as these.

Section

8

Icebreaker Games

These games will help your kids get past those awkward first moments and get acquainted.

Human Animals

Genesis 1:24-25
Energy Level

Medium Energy

Kids love animals, and this game uses that enthusiasm to help your students get to know one another better.

Supply List

- ☐ markers, one per child
- ☐ index cards, one per child
- ☐ masking tape
- ☐ craft materials: construction paper, fabric scraps, yarn, toilet paper, and so on

The Game

Divide students into groups of three to five, making sure all students are actively involved, with no bystanders.

Hand out markers and index cards to each group, one per child, plus a length of masking tape. Have each child quickly either write or draw a favorite animal on the card, along with his or her name, and ask kids to tape their cards to their shirts.

When this is finished, let students decide among themselves who will be the designated "model" for their group. Let kids discuss their favorite animals and why they like them, and then have them vote as a group to choose an animal to "create." Using available craft materials, the children in each group should create a costume around the model. The costume can be as simple or complex as time, supplies, and creativity allow. For example, a construction paper triangle and craft feathers could create a parrot. Floppy ears and a rope tail could make a dog. A yarn mane and tail could portray a horse. Time the activity based on your own time availability.

When time is up, have the models parade around the room showing off their groups' creativity.

Post-Game Discussion Questions

After playing this game, have the students sit down in their groups. The models should keep their costumes on during the discussion unless for some reason costumes are uncomfortable. Ask each group to respond to these questions in turn:

• **Why did you choose the animal you chose?**

• What was the hardest part about making your animal?

• Why do you think God made animals?

• What are some things you like about animals? What do animals do for us?

Say: **The Bible makes it clear that God wants us to enjoy and benefit from animals, as well as take care of them.**

What Animal Am I?

Genesis 2:19-20a

Energy Level

High Energy

In this game children will try to find out what animal name has been stuck to their backs by asking "yes" or "no" questions. In the process they'll learn that God made all the animals and Adam named them.

Supply List

☐ markers

☐ name tags or sticky labels, one per child

The Game

Before class write a different animal name on each label, one per student. Explain that each student will receive a sticker on his or her back with an animal name on it. They're not allowed to tell each other what animal they are, but must follow the rules of the game. Proceed to stick an animal name label on each student's back.

Say: **The only way you can find out what animal you are is to ask "yes" or "no" questions. For example, "Am I white and black?" or "Do I have floppy ears?" You may ask as many questions as you want, but you can only ask each person one question at a time. Each time you ask a new person a question, say your name and ask the person his or her name so we can all get to know each other better.**

You may want to demonstrate to the class how to play by allowing a volunteer to choose an animal for you to be. Proceed to ask "yes" or "no" questions to try to guess what animal you are.

Once a student guesses his or her animal, the student should make animal noises and act like the kind of animal he or she is.

When all students have guessed who they are, or time has run out, regroup and say: **God created many different kinds of animals. He had Adam name each one of them. What a fun job that must have been!**

Post-Game Discussion Questions

After playing this game, ask your students to sit down in groups of three and discuss:

• What animal were you? Describe your favorite thing about this animal.

• How easy or hard was it for you to guess what animal you were by only asking "yes" or "no" questions? Why?

• The Bible tells us that God gave Adam the task of naming each and every animal. Why do you think God made so many different animals?

Say: God made all the animals. Adam had the fun task of naming each one. As you enjoy the animals God created, remember to thank God for being so creative!

Just a Mask

1 Samuel 16:7
Energy Level

Low Energy

This game will demonstrate to kids that how they look has little to do with who they really are.

Supply List

☐ paper plates, one per child
☐ markers, crayons, pens
☐ craft sticks, one per person
☐ masking tape
☐ optional: craft supplies

The Game

Give each child a paper plate. Set out markers, crayons, and pens for kids to share. You can also supply craft items such as yarn, glitter glue, and fabric scraps for kids to use, if you wish. Have kids each make a face mask on his or her paper plate.

On the other side of the mask, have kids each write three things that they love. Finally, have kids each tape a craft stick handle to the back of the plate. Gather the masks, and scramble them in the center of the room. Have kids form a circle around the masks.

Let kids each choose a mask, making sure it's not their own. Go around the circle and have each child read what's written on the back of the mask. Let the rest of the class guess who the mask really belongs to.

Post-Game Discussion Questions

After playing the game, ask your students to sit down in groups of three and discuss:

• **How was trying to guess which mask matched which person like Samuel trying to figure out which of Jesse's sons God had chosen to be king?**

• **How is our outward appearance like a mask of who we really are?**

• **Do you think God cares how we look? Why or why not?**

• **How should we try to look at each other?**

Encourage kids to take their masks home to remind them that God looks at the heart, not at our outward appearance.

Blessing Ball!

Psalm 40:4

Energy Level

High Energy

In this game your kids will focus on how God has blessed them.

Supply List

❑ permanent markers, one for every five or six students

❑ beach balls, one for every five or six students

❑ fast-paced Christian music

The Game

As the students arrive, have them blow up the beach balls. Ask children to form groups of five or six.

Say: **You've all played Musical Chairs, but this is a bit different. While the music plays, you keep the beach balls in the air and the markers passing from one person to another within your groups. When the music stops, the** person who has the ball must say his or her name and one way God has blessed him or her. The person with the marker will write that blessing on the beach ball. Be sure you don't repeat any blessings. Ready? Go!

Start and stop the music yourself, several times, so that each person will likely get a turn to add a blessing to the beach ball.

Post-Game Discussion Questions

After playing this game, ask your students to sit down in their groups and discuss the following questions. Collect the markers so they won't be a distraction.

• Why is it sometimes hard to list the blessings God has given us?

• How can a Christian make blessing others a consistent part of his or her everyday life?

• How would the world be different if all we could say about each other would be positive things?

Remind your students that God's blessings are around them all the time! All they have to do is keep their eyes open and they'll be on the "blessing" ball.

Getting to Know You

Psalm 139

Energy Level

Medium Energy

This game will help your kids understand how unique and special each one of them is in God's eyes, while helping them get to know each other better.

Supply List

❏ pencils, one per student

❏ game grid—one per student (see below)

The Game

As you get to know your students throughout the year, make a mental (or written!) note of interesting qualities or details about each student.

For this game, use the facts you've gathered to create a game to help your students get to know each other. Create a simple grid, maybe 4x5 squares on a full sheet of paper. Then write one fact in each square. Each fact should be an interesting one that you know is true of at least one student. For example, some facts might include "This person has traveled to more than one foreign country," "This person can roll his or her tongue," or "This person owns a horse."

Make enough copies of the game grid for each person to have one. Distribute the grids and pencils. Challenge students to mingle and find people who fit the descriptions on the grid. Whenever they find someone, they should have that person sign that square on their grid.

Post-Game Discussion Questions

After playing this game, have the students sit down and discuss these questions:

• **How well did you know the people in our group?**

• **Why is it important to get to know each other?**

• **How well does God know us?**

Say: **Psalm 139 tells us that God knows each of us completely, and he loves us. We can get to know each other well too.**

Name Freeze

Psalm 147:4

Energy Level

Medium Energy

This game will help your kids learn that God knows each one of them by name.

Supply List

☐ beanbags, one per child (If you don't have beanbags, use resealable snack-size bags filled loosely with dried beans.)

☐ book with pictures of stars or galaxies (optional)

The Game

Read aloud Psalm 147:4, "He determines the number of the stars and calls them each by name." Then say: **Think about a time when you've looked at the sky at night. Think about how many stars there are.** If you live in a large city, there's a chance that children may not have had the experience of stargazing, so if you brought in a picture of stars, show it to the children now.

Do you think you could count all the stars? Or memorize all their names even if you could count them? None of us could do that, because there are more stars than we can see, even if we had the world's most powerful telescope! Yet the Bible tells us that God knows how many stars there are, and he knows the name of each one! That's because God made them all.

Guess what? God knows *your* **name too! And he knows everything about you. Let's play a game to help us learn each other's names. If it's important to God to know your name, then it's important to us to know each other's names.**

Give each child a beanbag. Instruct students to balance the beanbags on their heads without touching them as they move around the room. When a beanbag falls off, that child should stop moving and remain frozen in place. Kids "unfreeze" each other by calling the frozen person by name and placing the beanbag back on his or her head. (If they don't know someone's name, they should just ask.)

Vary the game by giving directions such as moving around the room by walking fast, twirling, skipping, or hopping (a hard one!).

Post-Game Discussion Questions

After playing this game, ask your students to sit down in groups of three and discuss:

• How do you feel when someone calls you by your name? Why?

• Why is it important for us to know each other's names?

• Name one or two people whose names you didn't know before.

• How does it feel to know that God knows you by name?

Say: **It feels good to know that God knows us by name, and it makes others feel good when we know their names too.**

Name Game

Proverbs 22:1

Energy Level

Low Energy

This game will help children get to know one another and be reminded that God gives each of us different interests and talents that make us special.

Supply List

☐ none needed

The Game

Have all the children stand in a circle. Say: **I'm glad that all of you are here. I'd like to teach you a game that will help us get to know one another.** As the adult leader, begin the game. Introduce yourself by telling your name and something about yourself (for example, an interest or hobby). You should also choose an action or hand motion that represents that quality. For example, you might say "I'm Pete and I like to play baseball" while pretending to swing a bat.

The child to your left will be next. She may say: "Pete likes to play baseball" while pretending to swing a bat, then "I'm Jessica, I love to read" while pretending to hold a book.

Play continues around the circle with each child recalling the name, interest, and action of the previous group members, introducing themselves and choosing an action. The last person will have to recall the whole group! It's OK for him or her to ask for help.

Be sure to include all adult leaders in this activity. Be prepared to help timid children think of a characteristic and motion. After everyone has had a turn, ask if anyone else would like to attempt to recall the whole group.

Post-Game Discussion Questions

After playing the game, have children sit down in the circle and discuss the following:

• **Why do you think God gave each of us different interests and abilities?**

• **Proverbs 22:1 says that a good name is more valuable than riches. What do you think it means to have a "good name"?**

• **How can you make sure that your choices and actions will give you a good name?**

Now that your children know a little more about each other, they'll feel more comfortable interacting!

Lion's Pride

Amos 3:3-4a
Energy Level
High Energy

In this game, students will learn about the impact their choice of who to help can have.

Supply List
❑ four slips of paper per student
❑ four baskets
❑ pencils for each student

The Game

Have each student write his or her name on four slips of paper and then place one slip in each basket. Set the baskets in four corners of the playing area. Tell each student to pick a name slip from a basket to start (but not his or her own name). Each student is to find and link arms with the person on the slip of paper in order to go to a basket and choose another name, putting the old slip into the basket. Before students begin, remind them to work together and carefully maneuver around the room.

Each child may link arms only with one person at a time and can find a new partner after he or she draws a new name from the basket. A person must be with another person in order to draw a name from the basket. Tell them to hurry and help anyone waiting to link arms with them, because only two people can be linked together at one time, and some kids may be waiting their turn to go to the basket. Pairs can go to any basket *not* in the corner where the pair links up. The object is to see how many kids each student can find as a partner in three to five minutes, helping as many people in the class as possible.

Post-Game Discussion Questions

After playing this game, ask your students to discuss:

• **What was the hardest part of the game?**

• **How did you choose who to walk with to the basket?**

• **Are the people we choose to be our friends the same people we choose to help most? Explain why or why not.**

• **How does God want us to choose who to help?**

One of a Kind

Mark 16:15-16

Energy Level

Medium Energy
This game will get kids talking to and learning about one another as they work to quickly get the same flavors of candy.

Supply List

☐ ten wrapped chewy candies per child, in assorted colors
☐ small sandwich bags, one per child

The Game

Ask a helper to assist you in quickly distributing ten wrapped candies of assorted colors to each child. Also give each child a small sandwich bag in which to hold the candies.

Say: **There are only two rules to this game. First, you will try to get ten pieces of candy that are the same color by trading with others. Second, you can only trade with someone else by telling that person one thing he or she doesn't know about you. For example, if I was trying to collect yellow, and** [name of child] **had a yellow candy to trade with me, I would tell** [name of child] **something about me, like my favorite sport.**

Ask children if there are any questions, then begin the game. When most children have all their candies of one color or are getting close, call time. Be careful not to make this game competitive. The goal is to learn about others, not to get the most pieces of like-colored candy. One way to stay away from competition is to stop the game before anyone has all one color.

Post-Game Discussion Questions

After playing this game, ask your students to find a partner who was trying to collect the same color of candy and discuss the following questions:

• **How did it feel to tell others something they didn't know? Why?**

• **What can we tell others that they might not know about God?**

• **Who can we tell about God's love and forgiveness?**

Say: **In our game, we went to our friends to tell them something new about us. In the Bible, Jesus told us to go into the world and tell others about God's love and forgiveness.**

Name Rhythm

John 10:3, 11
Energy Level
Medium Energy
This game will allow your students to share a unique thing about themselves with the group, as well as help students see that Jesus knows them each by name.

Supply List
☐ none needed

The Game

Gather students together. Have them hold hands and form a circle facing in.

Say: **To introduce ourselves we'll share something unique about ourselves, and a nickname we might want to be called. I'll go first.** Say something like, "My name is Mrs. Smith. I can play volleyball really well so you can call me 'Spike.' " Instruct the students to say, "Hi, Spike." Have the student to your left take a turn. The student may say something like this: "I'm Julie. I can wiggle my nose, so you can call me 'Wiggles.' " The group will then say, "Hi, Wiggles." Go around the circle until each person has shared his or her name and a nickname.

Next, play a rhythm game to help students practice saying everyone's name. Have students clap twice, pat their legs twice, clap twice again, then call out a name. Names can be real or a nickname provided. When a person's name is called, he or she must stay in rhythm and call out someone else's name. Play until everyone's name is called or time runs out. The adult leader will be in charge of keeping the game going and calling on students when the rhythm is disrupted.

Post-Game Discussion Questions

After playing this game, ask your students to sit down in groups of three. Say: **In this game we all got to know each other a little bit better. Jesus knows each of us by name. Isn't that awesome?** Have the groups discuss:

• **What was your favorite nickname for a classmate? Why?**

• **How easy or hard was it to remember everyone's name or nickname?**

• **The Bible tells us that Jesus, the good shepherd, knows each of our names. How does that make you feel about his care for you?**

Say: **Jesus knows us each by name! What kind of fun nickname might Jesus have for you?**

Bubble Buddies

Acts 2:44

Energy Level

High Energy

This game will help your kids get to know each other and understand what it means to have things in common, just like the early church.

Supply List

- ☐ bubble solution
- ☐ bubble wand

The Game

As the students arrive, say: **Watch closely while I blow some bubbles. Let's count them together, and then you get into groups with that many people and sit down. If you can't find that many people to form a group, then you get to come up here and be one of the Wise Ones.**

In your groups, tell each other your names, and answer the question that the Wise Ones will ask.

Blow the bubbles. If there are three in the air, then have the children form groups of three. If there are nine in the air, then a group or groups of nine need to form. As soon as the groups form, have the children introduce themselves to each other.

Have those who can't find a group with the appropriate number work together to come up with a question for the other groups to answer. They may ask the groups to describe their favorite pair of socks or what their favorite TV show is. Encourage them to be creative. The pressure is on, so they'll have to work fast. The Wise Ones can introduce themselves to each other while the other groups are answering their question. Repeat several times, watching that the same children are not repeatedly the Wise Ones.

Post-Game Discussion Questions

After playing this game, ask your students to sit down in groups of three and discuss:

- **Why do you think it can be hard to get to know somebody new?**
- **Why would church be a better place if everyone knew everyone else?**
- **Why would it be easier to be a Christian if you had a group of good friends who were trying to be good Christians too?**

Say: **The early church gathered together every day to share about Jesus and their lives. They understood the importance of sharing their lives and helping each other. We can do that too!**

My Nickname Could Be...

Acts 4:36; Mark 3:17
Energy Level

Low Energy

This game helps kids associate something positive about each other, as well as learn each other's names.

Supply List

☐ none needed

The Game

Invite the kids to sit in a circle. Say: **Some of you probably have nicknames. A nickname can be a** shorter or different version of your full name, or a nickname could have something to do with how you look, act, or think. You might like your nicknames— or you might not!

What if you could pick your own nickname? Think about something you like about yourself or something you like to do. It needs to be positive and something you'd want everyone here to know about. For example, if you really like basketball, you might say your nickname should be "Hoops Skyler." You may choose to give some more fictitious examples or choose a nickname for yourself to tell the class.

Give the kids a few moments to think about a nickname for themselves. Then let a volunteer begin with this sentence: "My name is _____ but my nickname could be _____ because..." briefly adding why that nickname is appropriate. For example, "My name is Jordan but my nickname could be Monster Truck because I like trucks and my dad took me to a truck show."

Then the next child has a turn. He first has to repeat the child's name already said along with the nickname and then add his own. The third child repeats the first two nicknames and then adds her own. Continue to play around the circle, letting kids help one another if someone forgets a name. For example, "That's Hoops Skyler, then Monster Truck Jordan, Read-a-Book Chris, Puppy-raising J.R., Christmas Casey, and my name is Taylor but my nickname could be Doctor because that's what I want to be when I grow up."

Play until everyone has had a turn. At the end, let volunteers try to name everyone, especially those kids near the end whose names were not repeated often.

Post-Game Discussion Questions

After playing this game discuss these questions with the kids:

• What did you learn about another person here from this game?

• Who here has something in common with you, based on his or her nickname?

• Who can you think of in the Bible that had a nickname?

Time Tenders

1 Corinthians 10:31
Energy Level

Low Energy

Children will get to know each other as they discover that God cares about how they spend their time.

Supply List

❑ one large sheet of poster board for every four to six children
❑ marker
❑ one beanbag for every four to six children

The Game

Before class, draw two lines on a large sheet of poster board, dividing it into four quadrants. In each of the quadrants, write one of the following phrases: "at school," "after school," "at home," and "at recess." Make a poster for every four to six children.

Place the posters on the floor. Have the children form groups of four to six around each poster, and take turns tossing a beanbag onto the poster. After tossing the beanbag, a child should say his or her name, the words the beanbag landed on, and then share one thing that he or she enjoys doing during that time. Repeat, giving all the children at least one turn.

After everyone has had a turn to share, get the children's attention, and read aloud 1 Corinthians 10:31, **"So whether you eat or drink or whatever you do, do it all for the glory of God." This verse means that no matter what time of day it is, there is always a way that we can honor God.**

Resume game play. This time instruct the children to name one way that they can please God during the time of day the beanbag lands on.

Post-Game Discussion Questions

After playing this game, gather the children together to discuss these questions:

• **Why is it important to honor God in everything we do?**

• **Are you surprised that there are so many ways to honor God? Why or why not?**

• **What is one new way that you can honor God this week?**

Say: **God made us so that we can honor God. No matter what we are doing and no matter what time it is, we can always find a way to honor God.**

We Can Do It!

1 Corinthians 14:12b
Energy Level

High Energy

This game will help students realize the importance of teamwork in the body of Christ.

Supply List

❏ index cards, each naming a skill or talent that one or more of your students might have, at least one card per student (it's OK to repeat some skills)

❏ several blank index cards

❏ clear tape or masking tape

The Game

Before class, prepare some index cards with skills or talents your students may have, being realistic for their age. For example: "I am good at math," "I am good at soccer," "I can bake chocolate chip cookies," or "I am a good listener." Depending on your students' ages and personalities, you might want to include some humorous or gross examples (which kids will love), such as "I can burp louder than anyone else." Also, for some skills that are common or popular, such as "I am good at math" or "I am good at video games," you may need to make up more than one card.

Gather your students, and introduce the game by saying: **Today we're going to play a game that helps us get to know each other better and celebrates the things our class can do.** Start by introducing yourself and naming one activity you enjoy. Encourage each child to introduce himself or herself to the others, naming a favorite activity. Some students will be modest or shy about naming their favorite activities, so be prepared with some suggestions. (Do you like to play with friends? Do you like to read books or watch movies?)

Have your students line up against one wall or divider in your classroom. Say: **It was fun to meet each other and discover some of the activities we enjoy. Now I'm going to read some things that we might be good at. If what I read is true for you, I want you to run past me, grab the card from me, and run to the other end of the room. As you gather there with the other kids, start working together using your cards to create a model of a church building.**

Gather your prepared index cards in a stack, and stand in the middle of the activity area. Begin reading from the cards, one at a time. A student who has that skill will run past you, take the card, and go to the other side of the room. If two or more students run past you for the same card, hand each one a card, having the students run in place as you hand out additional blank cards.

As students arrive at the other side of the room, they should use their index cards and the tape provided to build a model of a church building. When all the students have arrived at the other side of the room, and as they work together to create their church structure, ask:

• Who was good at math?

• Who makes good chocolate chip cookies?

• Who was good at video games?

• Who plays the piano?

Let students identify *by name* their peers who possessed each named skill, going through the list from the game so that by game's end they know each other's names well. Be sure to praise the work students have done on their model church.

Post-Game Discussion Questions

After playing this game, ask your students to sit down together for a discussion. Note that some answers may be the same for the first two questions.

• What are some activities you do by yourself?

• How about some activities that you do with other people?

• Why do some activities have to be done with more than one person?

• How can each person having different skills or abilities be a good thing?

• What are some ways you see people using their abilities in the church?

• How can we use the gifts that were listed on our cards to help the church?

Post It!

Ephesians 4:29
Energy Level
Medium Energy

This game will not only help your kids learn each others' names, but also help them learn how special each person in your group is.

Supply List
❑ large sheet of newsprint taped on the wall

❑ ten medium to large sticky notes for each student

❑ pen or pencil for each student

❑ bold marker

The Game

As the students arrive, write their names on the newsprint with a bold marker. Write them large, and spread around.

Say: **When reporters have a story they want to print, they post it. You are now reporters and you have to find your stories. Interview each other and report one good thing about the person you interview. As soon as you can, run to find that person's name on the newsprint. If no one else has reported your scoop on that person, post it!**

Write the fact on a sticky note, and stick it to the poster.

If your fact has already been reported, then you've been scooped and you have to go and find something else good about that person. No double scooping. You can only post a good news story about each person one time.

Distribute sticky notes and pencils or pens. Tell students to look for fun facts and unusual hobbies. They can also look for unique characteristics in people or in their families. They're reporters looking for a scoop, so they've got to dig deep and make it interesting!

The game ends when everyone is out of sticky notes. Be sure to give students a few minutes to peruse the poster after everyone's finished.

Post-Game Discussion Questions

After playing this game, ask your students to sit down in groups of three and discuss:

• What was the most surprising bit of news that you posted?

• How hard was it to stay positive in your reporting? Why?

• Why is it so hard to stay positive outside of this activity?

• How would the world be different if all we could say about each other would be positive things?

Rock. Paper. Scissors

Philippians 2:4
Energy Level
Low Energy
This game will help your kids discover that to really care for their friends, kids need to know what is happening in their friends' lives.

Supply List
☐ none needed

The Game

Say: **The Bible tells us, "Each of you should look not only to your own interests, but also to the interests of others"** (Philippians 2:4). **We're going to play a game called Rock, Paper, Scissors.**

Explain the rules of Rock, Paper, Scissors. Kids make a fist. Together they count one, two, three, and then with their hand they make one of three symbols. A fist represents rock; two fingers form scissors; and a flat, open hand represents paper. Rock beats scissors because rock can crush scissors; scissors beats paper because scissors can cut paper; and paper beats rock because paper can cover the rock.

Help the kids find partners. Say: **Now that you know how to play Rock, Paper, Scissors, go ahead and play. The winner must tell the other person his or her name, favorite food, and favorite television show.** After kids have played with their first partner, have them find another partner and repeat the game. Play long enough so each student has introduced him- or herself to at least four other people.

Post-Game Discussion Questions

After playing this game, ask your students to sit down in groups of three and discuss:

• **Which did you think was most fun, telling the other person about yourself or learning something about the other person? Why?**

• **Why is it important to learn the likes and dislikes of your friends?**

• **Why does God want us to care about our friends?**

Say: **The Bible makes it clear that we should be interested in others. To be a true friend, it's important to know what makes your friends "tick." It's important to know their likes and dislikes. The more you know about a friend, the easier it is to know how to help that person when he or she is feeling down.**

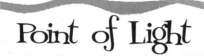

Point of Light

Philippians 2:14-15
Energy Level

Low Energy

This game will help your kids learn that by working together they can create something beautiful in Christ.

Supply List

☐ ball of yarn

The Game

When the children arrive, have them form a circle. Say: **Although we're special as individuals, God has also called us to be united in Christ. I'll start by holding the end of this yarn, and passing this ball of yarn to someone else in the group. As I do, I'll say something positive about the person I'm tossing the ball of yarn to.** Hold onto the yarn and toss the ball to a student across the circle. **My name is and what I like about** [the person's name] **is _____.**

Have each student hold their bit of yarn and pass the ball to another student, saying something good about that person. When everyone has had a turn to catch the yarn, say something nice, and pass the yarn to someone else, say: **Together we are a wondrously beautiful creation of God. Look at the beautiful star we made! It wasn't hard, and all it took was a little encouragement and working together.**

Post-Game Discussion Questions

After playing this game, ask your students to sit down in groups of three and discuss:

• **What was the hardest part about creating this star?**

• **Why is it important that we work together in the church?**

• **How does what we do make us shine like stars?**

Remind the kids that even though they can't always be connected by a beautiful star of yarn, they are always connected by the love of God, and that makes all the difference in the world.

Mustache Mania

Philippians 4:4

Energy Level

Medium Energy

Use this game to help your kids celebrate the joy that we have in the Lord.

Supply List

❑ two or three cosmetic eyebrow pencils

❑ paper

❑ pencils

❑ Bible

❑ feathers

The Game

Warmly greet students as they arrive. Distribute eyebrow pencils, and ask students to help each other draw funny mustaches on their faces. Help if needed, and be sure kids are doing a good job sharing the eyebrow pencils so everyone has a chance to participate.

When goofy mustaches are in place, challenge children to find out something new about each person in the group. Give each person a piece of paper and a pencil to write down what they learn about their classmates. Before they get started, issue this warning: No one is allowed to crack a smile at any time during the activity. Give each student a colorful feather (sold by the bagful in craft departments) to tickle classmates who can't conceal their joy!

Post-Game Discussion Questions

After several minutes of interaction, gather everyone back together. Ask a volunteer to read aloud Philippians 4:4. Then discuss the questions below.

• **What things make you laugh and smile?**

• **Why does loving God make us happy?**

• **What things can you be happy about even when other stuff isn't going very well?**

End the session by practicing lots of big smiles. You could even photograph your kids' winning grins for extra fun.

Cool Gift Show 'n' Tell

James 1:17

Energy Level

Low Energy

This game allows your students to use their creativity to describe what their imaginary gift box holds, and helps students see that all good gifts come from the Father above.

Supply List

☐ none needed

The Game

Tell students they each brought something for show 'n' tell. Say: **It's an imaginary gift box. We'll take turns describing for the group what each of our gift boxes looks like, as well as the cool item we have inside of it.**

Go first to demonstrate to the class how it's done. Imagine the students' surprise as you describe in detail about the kangaroo from Australia or the baby dinosaur egg you carefully packaged and brought in. Next, go around the group and give each student an adequate amount of time to describe in detail what his or her box looks like.

After the box has been described, have the student pretend to open it. After it has been opened, give the student a few moments to describe in detail what he or she has brought to class for show 'n' tell.

After all the students have had a turn to describe their item, say: **These show 'n' tell gift boxes all contained some cool and exciting items. I'm impressed how creative you are! God has given each of us many exciting gift boxes to open during our lives. James says, "Every good and perfect gift is from above." When good things happen or good gifts come your way, it is not just a coincidence...it's from God!**

Post-Game Discussion Questions

After playing this game, ask your students to sit down in groups of three and discuss:

• **What gift box description was most interesting to you?**

• **How easy or hard was it for you to come up with a creative idea for your gift box? Why?**

• **The Bible tells us, "Every good and perfect gift is from above" (James 1:17). How does it make you feel to know that God sends you gifts from heaven?**

Say: **God has some great gifts picked out for you. What a cool thing to look forward to!**

Strange People in a Strange Land

1 Peter 2:11-12
Energy Level
Low Energy

This game will help your kids discover that each one of them is unique, and that God has asked your students to be different from people who surround them.

Supply List
❑ pencils, one per student
❑ index cards, one per student

The Game

Distribute the pencils and index cards, one per person. Say: **Each of us has had something happen to us that was weird or strange or embarrassing. Write that event on your index card without anyone else seeing what you've written. Don't sign your name. Just a reminder, anything you write will be read out loud, so be sure that what you tell is OK for everyone to know. When everyone has finished, we'll** collect the cards and guess which event is about which person.

Collect the cards, and read each one out loud. Give your students time to guess who belongs to which event. The game is over when you've run out of cards. By the way, it's not really fair unless you put your own index card in the stack along with the children's cards!

Post-Game Discussion Questions

After playing this game, ask your students to sit down in groups of three and discuss:

• What was the strangest thing you heard about in this game?

• One strange event doesn't really make you strange or a stranger. What does?

• Have any of you traveled to a strange land where the customs seemed like they were from an alien planet? How did you feel?

• Why would God want us to be strangers in this world? After all, we were born here and we live here.

Say: **God doesn't want us getting too comfortable in this world. He wants us to be different, just as Jesus was different. We should try to be like Jesus, because we know that our real home is heaven.**

Section

2

Group Builder Games

Twenty games to help kids form lasting friendships!

Desert Survival Gear Relay

Exodus 16:1-3, 11-15; 17:1-2, 5-6

Energy Level

High Energy
This game will challenge kids to work together as they think through what life in the desert was like for the Israelites.

Supply List

❑ adult-size pair of sandals or shoes for each team

❑ oversized hat (or sunglasses) for each team

❑ one set of index cards per team, including at least one card per team member. Each card should name or picture something the Israelites may have had in the desert, such as cookware, clothing, sheep, cows, tambourine, cart, walking stick, and so on

❑ several more index cards for each team that name or picture items that would not have been in the desert, such as a CD player, a race car, or swim goggles

❑ three more index cards for each team that name or picture water, manna, and quail or meat

The Game

Divide children into small groups, and line them up as for a relay. Say: **When the people of Israel were traveling through the desert, they had to take their "survival gear" with them—and carry nothing unnecessary!** Have teams briefly brainstorm what they think the Israelites needed or had with them.

Shuffle together all the teams' index cards *except* the ones picturing water, manna, and quail/meat—keep those yourself.

Place the shuffled cards in one pile at the opposite end of the play area faceup, so children can easily see what's on the top card.

To begin the game, the first "Israelite" on each team puts on a sun hat or sunglasses (to provide shade from the desert sun) and oversized shoes (because walking in sand is difficult). At your signal, those players race to the pile of index cards, each choosing a survival gear card and racing back with it. Those players will then give the hats and shoes to the next players in line. Each team member runs the relay in turn, trying not to duplicate any survival gear cards his or her team has already accumulated.

Team members may call out suggestions to their players. If someone brings back a card the rest of the team thinks isn't necessary or is a duplicate, the player will run it back to the pile and choose another card.

Each team will keep its collected cards at the back of the line.

At some point, children will start commenting that there are no water, manna, or food cards. Whenever someone comments on this or asks you about it, give that team one of the water, manna, or quail/meat cards you're holding and say: **God *gave* the people of Israel their water, manna, and meat. They didn't have to bring it with them or work for it.**

If the kids need prompting to notice your cards aren't in the pile, give them hints by saying things like "I wonder what the Israelites ate and drank in the desert?" or "What is your team of Israelites going to eat and drink?" Give enough prompts so that each team ends up with those three cards.

Because the people of Israel trav-

eled together, all the teams "win." Encourage teams to offer ideas to each other as they play or trade cards as necessary until all the teams are equipped with the proper survival gear.

Post-Game Discussion Questions

After playing this game, ask your students to sit in groups of three and discuss:

• **How might the people of Israel have felt relying on God for their most important "survival gear"—water, manna, and meat? Explain.**

• **How did you help your teammates? How did they help you?**

• **How does working together with others make us able to "survive" in life—or even just do better?**

Jump the Jordan

Joshua 3:1, 14-17
Energy Level
High Energy
As they face a challenge, this game will have your kids working together and looking for ways to help one another.

Supply List
☐ two long ropes

The Game

Stretch out the two ropes across your game area, parallel to each other and a few inches apart. Tell the kids that this is the Jordan River, and have them all stand on one "shore." At your signal, ask all the kids to jump across the "river," being careful not to get their toes "wet" by touching the space in between the ropes. Widen the river a little by moving the ropes a couple of inches farther apart. Then have all the kids jump back over to the first side. Continue to widen the river, a little at a time, having the kids jump over it after each widening. (You may want to assign one child to stay at the opposite end of the ropes from you and help you move them to keep the game fast-paced.)

When the ropes are finally far enough apart that jumping across is a challenge, explain what will happen when someone "falls in." Any child whose foot touches in between the ropes has to stay in the river until rescued. Kids on the shore may become "life preservers" by stretching out a hand to the child stuck in the river. If the child is too far away to reach, encourage the class to figure out how to become a lifesaver chain, such as by holding hands or linking arms in the river to reach the stranded child. Encourage all the kids to stop jumping when someone falls in until that child is rescued.

Continue to gradually widen the ropes, and let those who wish keep trying to jump over. The kids who choose to stay on the shore should look for opportunities to be life preservers and pull out the kids who don't make it. Play until no one can jump as wide as the river and everyone is safely on a shore.

Post-Game Discussion Questions

After playing this game, ask your students to sit in groups of three and discuss:

• The people of Israel didn't have to jump over the Jordan River, as we did in our game, but how do you think they might have helped each other as they crossed?

• What can we do to help each other—here at church and in other places?

• How would you feel knowing that whenever you came to church there'd be other kids who'd be happy to see you and who would help you? Explain.

Noisy Safari

1 Kings 19:11-13
Energy Level

Medium Energy
This game will help your kids to listen to God's still small voice in spite of all the noise around them.

Supply List

❑ one noisemaker for each child (tambourines, small cymbals, hand bells, drums, blocks of wood, kazoos, pennies in a milk jug, and so on)

❑ Bible

❑ clean cloth blindfold

The Game

This game is loud and might work best in an outdoor setting. Before the children arrive, place a Bible somewhere in the playing area.

Explain that only one person has permission to talk during this game. He or she will give verbal directions to a blindfolded student whose job is to find the hidden Bible. The other students will be spaced throughout the play area and use their noisemakers to distract the blindfolded person. They can pretend to be wind, earthquakes, or fire, but they cannot touch the blindfolded person and they cannot talk. The person who's blindfolded is to find the Bible in spite of all the noise. Repeat several times, giving different students the chance to be or to guide the blindfolded person.

You might want to set up a maze or even an obstacle course that the blindfolded person must get through before he or she can reach the Bible. Use items in your classroom for children to go around, under, and in between.

Post-Game Discussion Questions

After playing this game, ask your students to sit down as a group and discuss:

• **What made it difficult to hear and follow the directions you received?**

• **What noises or distractions do you hear in your life?**

• **How can we listen for God in the midst of all those distractions?**

Say: **One way to listen for God's voice is to take time every day to focus on only God and listen for him.**

Here Comes the Sun

Psalm 118:24

Energy Level

Low Energy

Children will get to know each other, make colorful sunbursts, and praise God.

Supply List

❏ one roll of yellow or orange crepe paper streamer for every ten children

❏ one bright balloon for every ten children

The Game

Have the children gather in groups of about ten. It's OK if you end up with some groups that are slightly larger or smaller. Read aloud Psalm 118:24: **"This is the day the Lord has made; let us rejoice and be glad in it."** This verse tells us that there is always a good reason to worship God. Let's make fun sunbursts to remind us that *this* is the day that God has made. No matter what's going on in our lives, there's always a good reason to worship God!

Give one child in each group a roll of crepe paper streamer. Say: **When you're holding the roll, tell everyone your name. Then say one reason it's a good day to worship God. You can tell about something you're thankful for, or you can share something that's awesome about God. Hold onto the streamer with one hand when it comes to you, then gently pass the roll to someone on the opposite side of the circle. Make sure you give the streamer to someone who hasn't had a turn yet.**

Let the children keep passing the streamer roll until the whole roll is used up. Then say: **Wow! You've made a sunburst! Let's play a game with these sunbursts. I'm going to toss an inflated balloon on your "sun." Work together to keep your balloon in the air with your sunburst. Be very gentle with your sunbursts—they will tear if you're rough with them.**

Start the game. If a balloon falls to the ground, help the group out by picking up the balloon and setting it in the middle of the sunburst. After several minutes, stop the game. Have each group carefully place its sunburst on the floor and sit around it in a circle.

Post-Game Discussion Questions

Have the children discuss these questions:

• How is keeping the balloon in the air like trying to keep a thankful, glad attitude?

• What kinds of days make it easy to be glad and thankful to God? What makes it hard?

• Why is it important to always be thankful to God?

Say: **Sometimes we have good days, sometimes bad. But no matter what happens, we can always be thankful to God. God is so awesome that there is always a new reason to praise him—even when life is hard.**

Trust Relay

Ecclesiastes 4:9-12

Energy Level

Medium Energy

As they work together to achieve a shared goal, your students will discover the importance of trust.

Supply List

❑ deck of playing cards with face cards removed

❑ four clean blindfolds

The Game

Remove the face cards from a deck of playing cards, leaving the aces in for the number one. Before students arrive, place these cards around the classroom, mixing them up randomly. These can be placed in plain sight.

When students arrive, invite them to play this "trust relay" game with you. Divide students into no more than four groups with a minimum of three students each. It's OK if you only have one or two groups. Ask for a volunteer from each group. Explain that the volunteer will be blindfolded, while the remaining children in each group will help the volunteer find a set of cards.

Say: **Volunteers, there are ten cards in each set, and your job is to find these cards and put them in order.** Assign each group one suit of the cards to find: hearts, diamonds, spades, or clubs. **The rest of the kids in your group must help you find them. Can you trust your helpers?**

Working at the same time, give the groups several minutes to find their sets of cards. The helpers can talk with the blindfolded volunteers and guide them around obstacles and other groups as well as tell the volunteers where to pick up the cards, but the volunteers must actually pick up each card. Depending on how much time you have, students could either be required to actually find the cards in order or to simply find them all and then place them in order with the helpers' guidance. The idea is not that they find the cards the most quickly, but that they do find all of them and bring them to you in the correct order when finished.

If time allows, kids can hide the cards again, and different students can take a turn being the blindfolded volunteers.

Post-Game Discussion Questions

When everyone has had a turn to be blindfolded, or when you're out of time, bring students back together in new small groups. Ask the following questions, giving the groups time to discuss each one:

• **What was hardest about this game? What was easiest? Why?**

• How did it feel having to trust the helpers on your team? How easy would it have been to find the cards by yourself?

• This game was one example of working together to achieve a goal. What are some other examples of times when working together is better than working alone?

Blind Man Safari

Isaiah 11:6-9
Energy Level
Medium Energy

As your children explore an animal maze and work as a unit, this game will help them discover God loves and cares for them.

Supply List
❏ stuffed animals or pictures of these animals, one each: wolf, lamb, leopard, goat, calf, lion, cow, bear, and snake

❏ clean blindfolds, one for every two children

The Game

Before children arrive, place stuffed animals or pictures of animals randomly around the room. Set up a maze, using chairs, books, or boxes, that passes by each of the animals.

Have the children form pairs or trios. Each pair or trio will blindfold one student. Students not wearing blindfolds will try to lead their blindfolded partners to each of the animals by using only their voices. The sighted students can give verbal directions—such as, go straight, turn left, put your right hand on the floor—but they can't touch the blindfolded partner.

The object is for the blindfolded children to find all the animals with the help of the group. Let one group begin, then wait a minute or two before starting the next group in the maze. After all the groups have finished, repeat the game, with different children blindfolded this time.

Post-Game Discussion Questions

After playing this game, ask your students to sit down in different groups of three and discuss:

• How were you able to find the animals in this game?

• What are some other ways to lead people besides speaking?

• How have you seen God use children to lead others? Explain.

Say: **God uses children as well as adults to do his work in the world. How might God use you during this week?**

All Strung Up

Jeremiah 18:1-6
Energy Level
Low Energy

This game will help your students think about how God shapes their lives, as they work together to create shapes from yarn.

Supply List
- ☐ ball of yarn
- ☐ scissors
- ☐ Bible

The Game

Greet your students as they arrive, and form small groups of four or five. Give each group a piece of yarn or string, ten to twelve feet long. If you'd rather keep your entire group together, use a monstrous piece of yarn twenty or thirty feet long. Either way, you'll need a large open play area.

Next, explain that you'll name an object and the kids will work together in their groups to form the shape out of the yarn. Start with some easy objects, like an orange, a book, and a heart. Then move on to more challenging objects—a house, a tree, a hat, a rabbit, a fish, a truck, or a flower.

Post-Game Discussion Questions

After students have worked together to form the outlines of several objects, gather everyone together. Read aloud Jeremiah 18:1-6. Then discuss these questions:

• **How was the game we played like the verses I just read?**

• **What does God use to shape us?**

• **What does God want us to be like?**

• **How can even bad things that happen to us help us become more like Jesus?**

Close by challenging your kids to think about how their lives are shaping up!

Bible Verse Hide 'n' Seek

Luke 11:9-10
Energy Level
Low Energy
This game will get children excited about exploring God's Word as students seek puzzle pieces and fit them together to form Bible verses.

Supply List
❏ brightly colored poster board, one sheet per ten to twelve children, with Luke 11:9-10 written on them
❏ marker with broad tip

The Game

Before the children arrive, write the words to Luke 11:9-10 (or any passage your group is studying) on a piece of poster board, large enough to cover the sheet. Cut the poster board into as many as twelve simple puzzle pieces. Hide the pieces all around the play area, using masking tape when necessary.

When children arrive, say: **Today we're going to play Bible Verse Hide 'n' Seek. I have hidden [number, color] puzzle pieces around the room. You need to work together to find the pieces, complete the puzzle, and read the Bible passage.** Give children boundaries if necessary, and send them to find the pieces. Encourage each child to find only *one* piece. Once a child has found a piece, that child should return to the appointed area to begin working the puzzle.

After children have completed the puzzle, have them read the verse or passage aloud together.

If you have a large group of children, you may make several posters, each one a different color. Posters can also feature different verses. Gather children in groups according to the color of puzzle pieces they find. If you use this option, be sure to emphasize that this is *not* a race but a group effort to seek God's message for us!

Post-Game Discussion Questions

After children have completed the puzzle(s) and read the verses, use the following questions to help them further explore the Scripture.

• **How would you say this verse in your own words?**

• You were very excited about finding and reading this Bible verse. How can we get excited every time we read God's Word?

• How is looking up a verse in the Bible like playing Bible Hide 'n' Seek?

Say: **Seeking God's Word and his message for us is exciting and rewarding!**

Blindfolded Search for Light

John 8:12
Energy Level

Medium Energy

Through this game the kids will search through "darkness" to find the light of Jesus and tell this good news to the others.

Supply List

☐ clean blindfolds, one per student

The Game

Have the kids spread out around the play area. Explain: **Jesus said that until we become friends with him, it's like we're walking around in darkness. But once we find him, it's like being in the light. In this game, we'll walk around in "darkness" and then help the others find the light.**

Help kids put on blindfolds. Secretly choose one child to be the Light-bearer, silently remove his or her blindfold, and have that child stand still.

Tell the rest of the kids to slowly walk around the room, gently bumping into things and each other, searching for the secret Light-bearer. Whenever two kids meet, they're to whisper to each other, "How do I leave the darkness?" If both ask the same question, they separate and keep on walking. But when someone bumps into the Light-bearer, they hear the whispered answer, "Jesus gives the light of life." That's the signal for that player to remove his or her blindfold and become a Light-bearer as well, linking arms with the original Light-bearer. Now, whenever someone bumps into either one of them, they both whisper the Light-bearer's answer.

As more kids find the Light-bearer and link with that group, the whispered message will become louder, giving a clue to those still wandering. Play until all the kids have become part of the Light-bearer group.

Post-Game Discussion Questions

After playing this game, ask your students to sit in small groups and discuss:

• **What helped you find the Light-bearer in our game?**

• **How is Jesus a light in your life?**

• **How could you work together with a friend or our church to be a light-bearer to others?**

End the session by challenging students to become light-bearers for others.

Human Obstacle Course

Acts 14:21-22; 2 Corinthians 11:23-28

Energy Level

Medium Energy

The kids will help each other in pairs as they explore obstacles faced by Paul.

Supply List

☐ none needed

The Game

Begin by saying: **When Paul traveled around to tell about Jesus, he faced many obstacles. Let's make an obstacle course—using just our bodies—that we can travel through in pairs.**

Brainstorm with the whole group ways a pair of kids could "become" an obstacle. For example, a pair could become an archway to walk under by pressing hands together up high. Other pairs could become a swinging gate to push through by stretching out arms, logs to step over by lying on the floor, or soldiers to duck past by swinging arms like swords. After brainstorming, divide kids into pairs, and let each pair choose a different obstacle to become.

Once all the pairs have figured out their obstacles, spread them out in a circular path around the room. Have one pair at a time leave their spot to walk through the obstacle course. When they've completed the course, they return to their spot to become an obstacle again, and another pair gets a turn. Encourage the partners to look for ways to help each other through the obstacles. Play until all have had a turn to travel through the obstacle course.

Post-Game Discussion Questions

After playing this game, ask your students to sit in small groups and discuss:

• **How did it feel to try to get through all these obstacles? Explain.**

• **What are some obstacles you remember Paul faced?**

• **How do you think Paul felt, traveling from city to city and facing obstacles? Explain.**

• **What are some ways we can help each other get through obstacles, or things that hold us back?**

Say: **Spreading the word about Jesus won't always be easy—sometimes we might face obstacles. But we can work together to help each other through those obstacles.**

Do Your Part

Romans 10:13-15

Energy Level

Medium Energy

This game will help kids see that they have a responsibility to share their faith with others.

Supply List

❏ none needed

The Game

Have kids form groups of four. In each group, assign the following body parts: one child will be the torso, one the head, one the arms and hands, and one the legs and feet.

Explain that you're going to give each "body" a task to do. Group members must work together to perform the task, but each person may only perform his or her *specific* body part's movements. (If you have a large class, give all groups the same task to try simultaneously. If you have a smaller class, let groups take turns performing different tasks.)

Suggest that groups perform the tasks of marching in place, doing jumping jacks, or moving a book from one spot to another. Group members should position themselves close together so they can perform their various bodily functions. Remind kids that the head, or brain, always needs to perform first.

After all groups have performed, lead the class in a round of applause for everyone's participation.

Post-Game Discussion Questions

After playing the game, ask your students to sit down in their groups and discuss:

• **Was performing your group's task harder or easier than you expected? Explain.**

• **What would have happened if one person in your group had refused to do his or her part?**

• **How is that like if one Christian refuses to share his or her faith or tell others about Jesus? What might happen then?**

Explain that we all have a responsibility to tell others about Jesus. If we refuse to do our part in the body of Christ, someone might never hear and become a follower of Jesus.

Marble Chute Continuum

Romans 12:4-8
Energy Level
Low Energy
Use this game to help kids see that the parts of the body of Christ work together to get things done.

Supply List
❏ one cardboard tube per child, any size (these could be from paper towels, gift wrap, and so on)
❏ one marble

The Game

Gather all the children in one large circle, shoulder to shoulder, and ask them to sit. For this game, the more kids in the circle, the better!

Give each child a cardboard tube. Show kids the marble, and tell them that they are to work together to get the marble all the way around the circle without dropping it. The only way they are allowed to do this is by tipping the cardboard tube just enough so it rolls through to the person on the

right. That person should be ready to receive the marble in one end of his or her cardboard tube, then pass it on to the next person. If the marble falls, the child will use the tube to pick it up and keep going—it's OK for two children to work together to pick up the marble. Make sure everyone understands the directions, give the marble to a child who will start, then call out: **Ready? Go!**

When the marble gets all the way around the circle, you may choose to play again or move on to the discussion questions.

Post-Game Discussion Questions

After playing this game, ask your students to sit down in groups of three and discuss:

• **How did it feel to work together to accomplish your goal? Explain.**

• **As Christians, how can we work together to help others know Jesus?**

• **Our bodies work together to keep us alive. In this game we were like a body, keeping the marble moving. How else are Christians like a body?**

Say: **Jesus wants us to work together to help others know about him. When we work together with our talents and abilities, God will do amazing things through us!**

Goofy Group Balloon Burst

1 Corinthians 12:4-11

Energy Level

High Energy

As they endeavor to pop balloons under a blanket, kids will have to work together to get the job done.

Supply List

❏ large blanket or sheet (the bigger the better), one per eight kids

❏ inflated balloons (eight or more per group, depending on the size of the blanket and of your group)

The Game

Plan on using one blanket and eight to ten balloons per eight kids.

Divide kids into groups of eight, give or take a few. Give each group a blanket and eight to ten inflated balloons. Explain that on your signal, they'll need to stuff all their balloons under the blanket and work as a team to pop them. The balloons *must* be under the blanket to be popped. Observe how the groups function together, and compliment those working cooperatively. Encourage those not yet functioning collectively to try to work together.

Post-Game Discussion Questions

After playing this game, ask your students to join you in discussing the game:

• **How did your group work together to pop your balloons?**

• **How would this game have worked if you had to pop all the balloons alone?**

• **Can you think of other ways a group could work together to get this job done?**

Say: **Even though each of us has different skills, we can get a job done better when we find ways to work together.**

Bridging the Gap

1 Corinthians 12:12-26

Energy Level

Medium Energy

This game will help children understand that God made everyone unique, and everyone has an important part to play. This is an excellent game to involve students with disabilities.

Supply List

❑ none needed

The Game

The object of this game is for kids to connect in such a way as to be able to touch two walls of a gymnasium or large room at the same time. One person starts by touching a wall with a body part (hand, foot, elbow), and thereafter the children must connect to each other to reach to the opposite wall. Every person has to be involved, and kids can get creative on how to reach the other side of the gym.

If the kids get stuck, you may offer this hint: Kids don't have to be *physically* touching each other—they could use sweaters, shoelaces, jackets, socks, and so on to bridge the gaps. Allow kids time to figure this out, and only give hints if they are really stumped!

Your role in this activity is that of a guide. Once the directions have been given, sit back and watch to see how the kids respond. If five minutes pass without any progress being made, give the students some hints as to how this task can be accomplished. Only give directions in small doses. Let the kids try to figure this out on their own as much as possible.

Post-Game Discussion Questions

After playing this game, ask your students to sit down and discuss:

• **What helped you most to accomplish this goal?**

• **Are there other ways to accomplish the same goal with fewer people?**

• **Who was the most important person in this game?**

Say: **In this game, everybody was equally important. Everyone was able to help achieve the goal. How is that like how God wants us to treat others who are different from us?**

Sitting Circles

1 Corinthians 12:27

Energy Level

Medium Energy

As your kids play this game, they'll discover the importance of working together as a whole—and why that's important in the body of Christ.

Supply List
☐ none needed

The Game

Have kids form a circle facing inward and touching shoulder to shoulder. Then have everyone turn to the right so that they are standing behind the person next to them. Say: **Our first task is to form a sitting circle. Once we do that, I'm going to give you a job to do. You must do the job staying connected** with everyone else in the group.

Instruct everyone to *slowly* sit down on the knees of the person behind him or her until everyone is sitting in a circle. This may require several tries! If your group is large, you may form more than one circle or challenge kids to form one huge circle.

Once the circle is formed, say: **Good job, everyone! Now let's exercise a few body parts without breaking the circle. Nod your head at me.** Pause. **That was too easy! Wave your right hand at me.** Pause. **I can see you're ready for something a lot tougher. Kick your right leg out to the side and back again.**

Respond according to what happens to the circle. If you want, make up a few more silly instructions. Then say: **Now for a real job! Are you ready?**

Give the group a task to accomplish, such as moving together to turn off the classroom light or to pick up a piece of paper on the floor and throw it away. Kids must move as a group. If someone falls off the circle, the entire group must stop and wait until everyone is seated again. The job isn't considered finished unless it's done with everyone seated in the circle.

Post-Game Discussion Questions

After playing this game, ask your students to sit down in groups of three and discuss:

• **Was it easy or hard to stay seated and move together as a group? Explain your answer.**

• How important was each person in playing this game? Explain.

• How does it feel to know that your part in God's kingdom is important? Explain.

Say: **Each of you is important to make the body of Christ work in the best way possible!**

Ultimate Set-Up Volleyball

Ephesians 4:16
Energy Level
High Energy

Through each child doing his or her part, the class will play a successful team game that sheds light on how to be the body of Christ.

Supply List
❑ beach ball or large balloon
❑ masking tape

The Game

Plan a game area large enough for all the kids to spread out, and remove any obstacles. Create a simple volleyball "court" by designating a centerline with masking tape on the floor. The side and end boundaries are not important.

Bring the kids to the playing area, and say: **Most team sports require teamwork. Today's game is like that. But this game just won't work if we don't work together—because there's only one team playing!**

Have all the kids stand on the same side of the volleyball court. Explain that in volleyball, players often "set up" the play by hitting the ball to another player on their own team rather than always trying to be the one to hit the ball over the net. In the ultimate setup of this game, everyone on the team "sets up" the ball (hits it) before it goes to the other side.

Serve the ball to the side with all the kids. One at a time, in any order, a student should hit the ball straight up in the air, keeping it on the same side of the court. After a child hits the ball, he or she immediately runs to the other side of the court. The last child on the first side gets to hit the ball across the line to the other side before running across. The game repeats on the second side, with every child hitting the ball before it is hit across the line.

Challenge the kids to see how long they can keep the volley going. Encourage them to aim when they hit so that another child can easily have his or her turn. If the ball touches the floor, start a new volley.

Post-Game Discussion Questions

After playing this game ask your students to sit in small groups and discuss:

• How did we each do our part in this game to make it work well?

• How is this game like being part of the body of Christ?

• How can you do your part in the body of Christ?

Marshmallow Surprise

Ephesians 4:25b

Energy Level

Low Energy
Students will learn that they are
part of the body of Christ as they
work together to create marshmallow models.

Supply List
- ❏ marshmallows
- ❏ toothpicks
- ❏ towel or box

The Game

Before class create a "model" using toothpicks and marshmallows. The model shouldn't be complicated and could be a replica of a small animal, a snowman, a house, and so on. Hide the model in a separate area of the room, under a towel or in a box.

Divide the class into groups of three to five students. Each group will choose one person to be its Translator. Invite all the Translators up to have a look at your marshmallow model, but keep it out of the sight of other children. Then send them back to their groups, where they must instruct their teammates—using only words—how to re-create the model they saw. The Translator may talk, but not draw, gesture, or touch the supplies. The groups should use the marshmallows and toothpicks you've supplied to re-create the model the best they can, based only on what they've been told by the Translator. After all the teams have finished, compare their models with the original to see if anyone came close to re-creating it. Be encouraging about how each team worked together and did their best to re-create the model.

Post-Game Discussion Questions

After playing this game, ask your students to form new groups and discuss these questions:

• **How easy or hard was it for you to create the model based only on what the Translator said? Why?**

• **Translators, what was hardest about your job? Explain.**

• **Teamwork is important in the Christian life. Give some examples of how Christians can work together as one body to complete a goal.**

Say: **God places great value on teamwork. Teamwork not only makes a task easier, but also helps each of us use our talents and gifts the way God desires. Just as we couldn't create the model on our own, we also need each other as Christians.**

Targets of Faith

Ephesians 6:10-18
Energy Level

Medium Energy

This game will help your kids work together to receive the whole armor of God.

Supply List

❑ six targets made from Hula Hoop plastic hoops, trash cans, masking tape, poster board, and so on

❑ symbols or pictures, two each of the following: belt, breastplate, boots, shield, helmet, and sword

❑ beanbags, one per child

Note: You can make a temporary beanbag by placing beans or pebbles in a sturdy, resealable sandwich-sized plastic bag. Double-bag for safety!

The Game

The object of this game is for a team to collect one piece of "armor" from each target to complete the whole armor of God. You may have all the children work together, or form them into two teams.

Place six targets around the room. Each target should have two pictures or symbols, both representing the same piece of armor. Every target will have pictures or symbols of a different piece of armor. For example, one target will have belts, another will have helmets, and so on.

Children will take turns tossing a beanbag at a target and then going to the end of the line. They'll continue to toss at the target until someone lands a beanbag inside the trash can or plastic hoop. When someone does that, that child should run to the target and collect the piece of armor from it for his or her team. If everyone takes a turn and no one makes it in the target, the last person to throw the beanbag should run and collect all the beanbags while another child collects the piece of armor for his or her team. Then the entire team moves on to the next target. The game ends when each team has collected all six pieces of armor.

Post-Game Discussion Questions

After playing this game, ask your students to sit down together and discuss:

• **Why do we need each piece of armor?**

• **What does it mean to be "strong in the Lord"?**

Say: **God's army needs kids like you!**

Standing Firm Challenge

Philippians 1:27
Energy Level
Medium Energy
Children will be challenged to work together and cooperate to keep themselves standing firmly in a small space.

Supply List
☐ Hula Hoop plastic hoops, large cardboard boxes, or masking tape

The Game

Create a space for a group to stand inside of. It can be inside a plastic hoop, a large cardboard box flattened on the floor, or a circle or other shape marked off with masking tape. One group or several can play this game simultaneously; each group needs its own space to stand in.

The challenge is for the people in each group (six to twelve, based on the size of the space) to work with one another so they all fit in the space—it will be tight!—and then sing a song while maintaining their position. Once everyone is in the space, one person sings the first line or phrase of a song, then the next person continues. The group must stay within the boundaries of the space until the song is finished. Song possibilities are "Jesus Loves Me," "This Little Light of Mine," "Row, Row, Row Your Boat," or "Twinkle, Twinkle, Little Star."

Space too easy to occupy? Tighten it and start again!

Post-Game Discussion Questions

After playing this game, ask your students to talk about it. Use these questions as discussion prompts:

• **In what ways did your group have to work together to play this game?**

• **If you had to do it again, what could your group do to make it easier to stand firmly in your little space?**

• **How can we honor God as a church by standing firm and working together?**

Say: **God is honored when Christians stand firm in their faith and work together.**

Putting Our Legs Together

Philippians 3:12-14

Energy Level

High Energy

This game will help your kids understand that God wants them to work together and help each other as they "run the race."

Supply List

❑ eighteen-inch lengths of rope or twine, one per person

❑ scissors (for leader)

The Game

D ivide your group into two groups. Have one group line up on one end of the room (or outdoors), and have the other group line up on the opposite end of the room, facing the first group.

Explain that students are going to participate in a many-legged race. They'll take turns running back and forth across the room. Each time a person or group gets to the other side, they'll add a person, who will have his or her ankle tied to the ankle of the last person in line. They'll need to move together back to the other side of the room.

Give each person, except for the first person in one line, a piece of twine. Have the person without twine run to the other side and tie one of his or her ankles to one ankle of the first person in the other line. Then have the two run back to the first side of the room together. The next person in line should tie one of his or her ankles to one of the "free" ankles in the pair. Then have the trio run to the other side and use another piece of twine to tie on the next person. Have students continue in this way until everyone is tied together.

It might be wise to have scissors or other sharp object available to help any students who cannot untie their twine at the end of the game.

Post-Game Discussion Questions

After playing this game, have the students sit down together, still tied at the ankles, to discuss these questions:

• **What was it like to work together in this way? Why?**

• **Why was it important to work together as you ran this race?**

Say: **We have another race to run— the race of life. In Philippians, Paul tells us that we need to run the race with perseverance, meaning that we don't give up. If we are there to help and encourage each other throughout the race of life, we will find the race much easier.**

Help the students untie all the twine.

Scripture Index

Energy-Level Index

High-Energy Games